Stories in the Heavens:

Constellations

Printed in 2022

St. Augustine's HEP
Catholic & Classical Liberal Arts Program
staugustineshep.com

ST. AUGUSTINE'S was founded to unite the best of the modern home school with the tradition of a Catholic liberal arts education. The goal of Catholic liberal arts education is to understand how everything humans can ever know fits together in a coherent image of God's universe and how He wants us to live in it. Such learning must be lived and carried into the heart as well as the mind.

Since love and knowledge grow together, Literature and History are at the heart of our curriculum. These subjects detail man's greatest hopes, and loves, and failings, when taught at any grade level.

Beyond ideas are the great men and women whose lives change millions of others by their correspondence to grace. When we come to know man's history, we are humbled and inspired by how God provided for our ancestors, both by revelation and the natural law. We learn to admire their greatness even while we are cautioned by their errors, for they tell us so much about our own time.

Summer Triangle

Summer Triangle

How to Draw Lyra

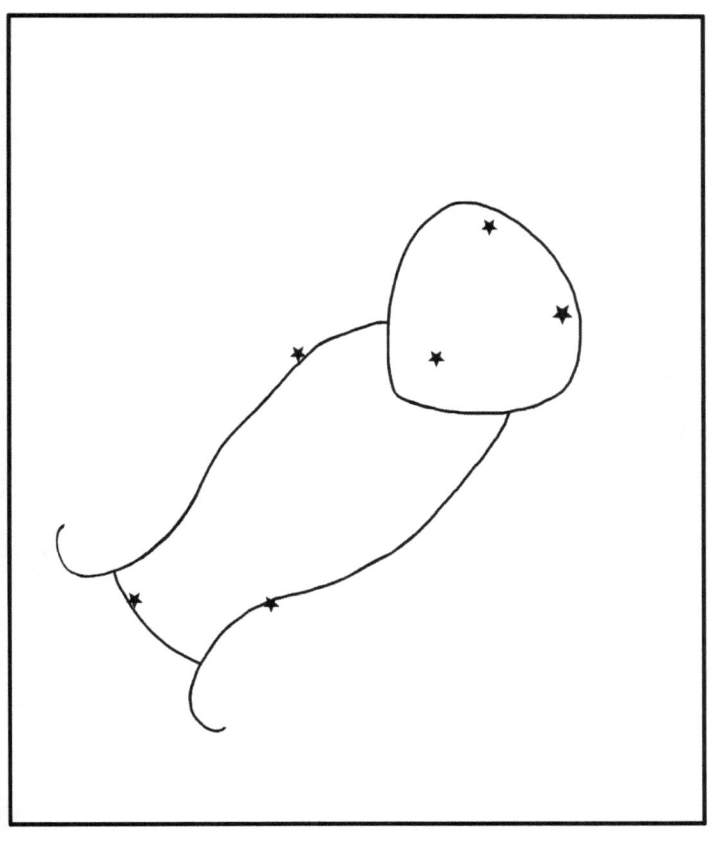

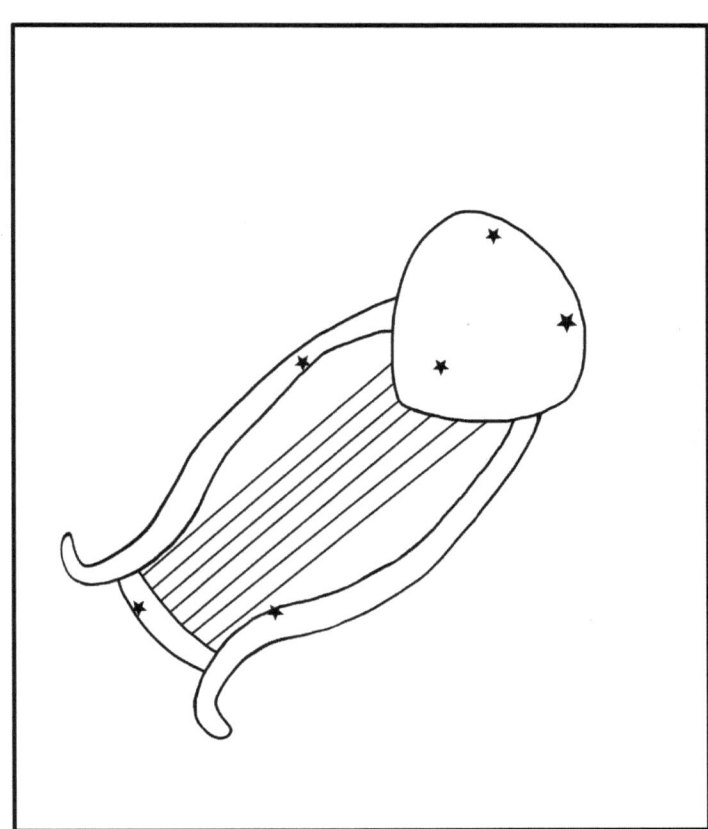

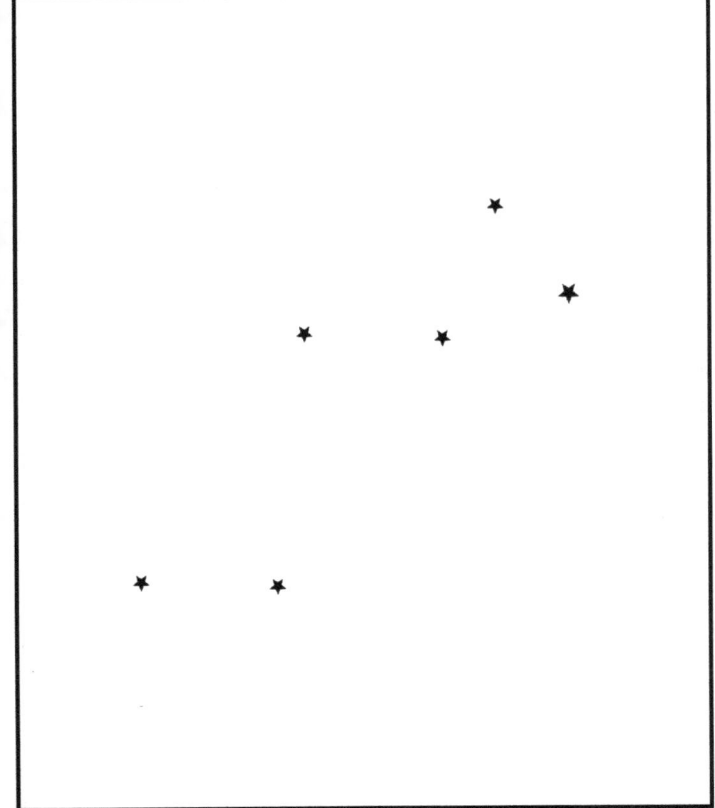

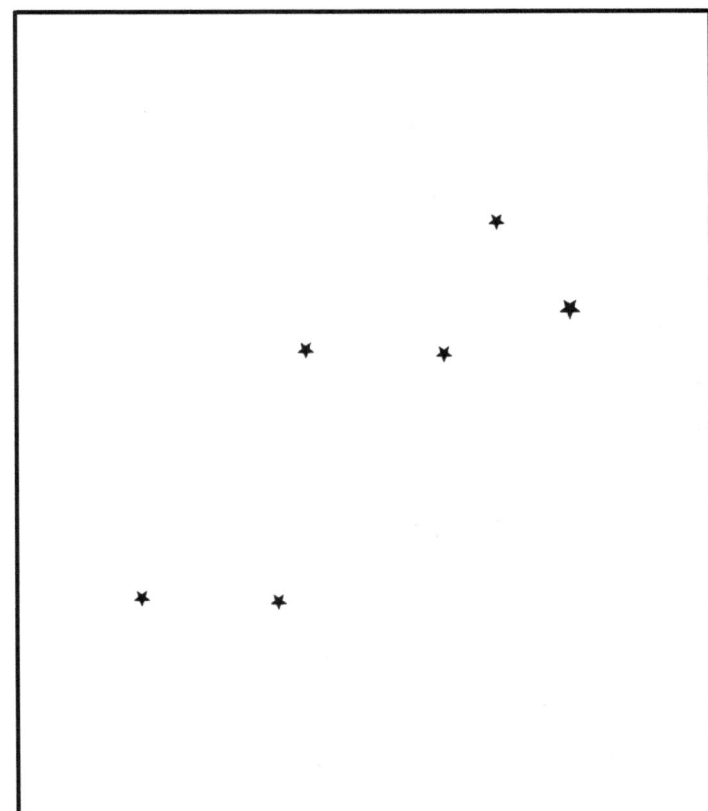

How to Draw Cygnus

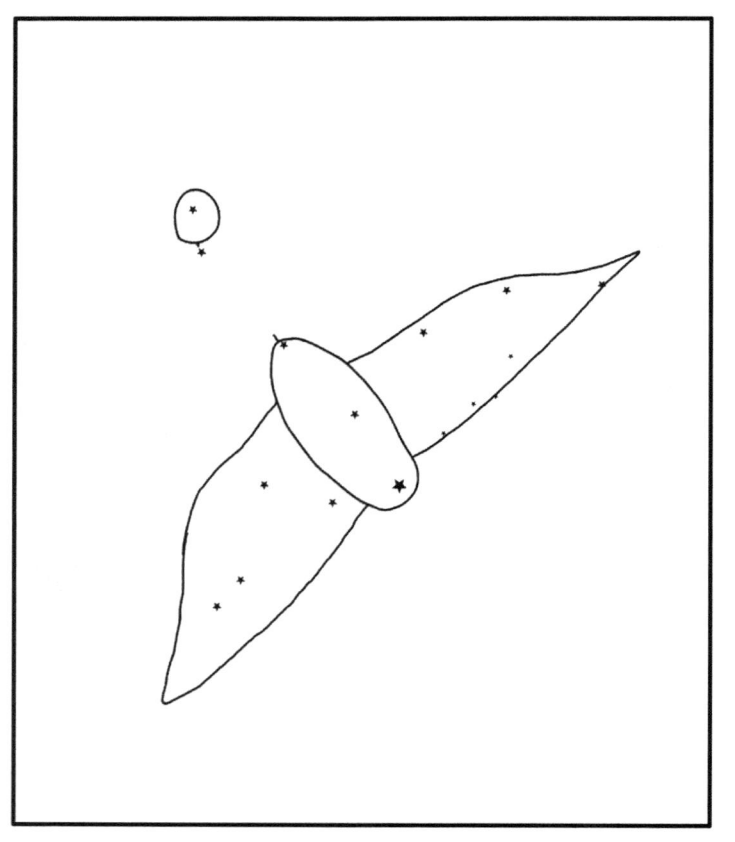
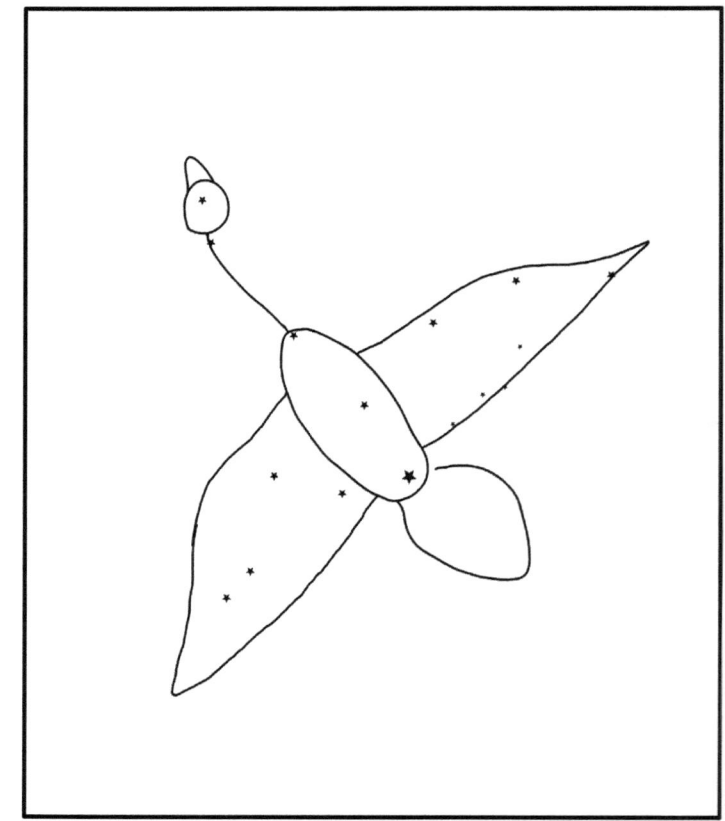

How to Draw Aquilla

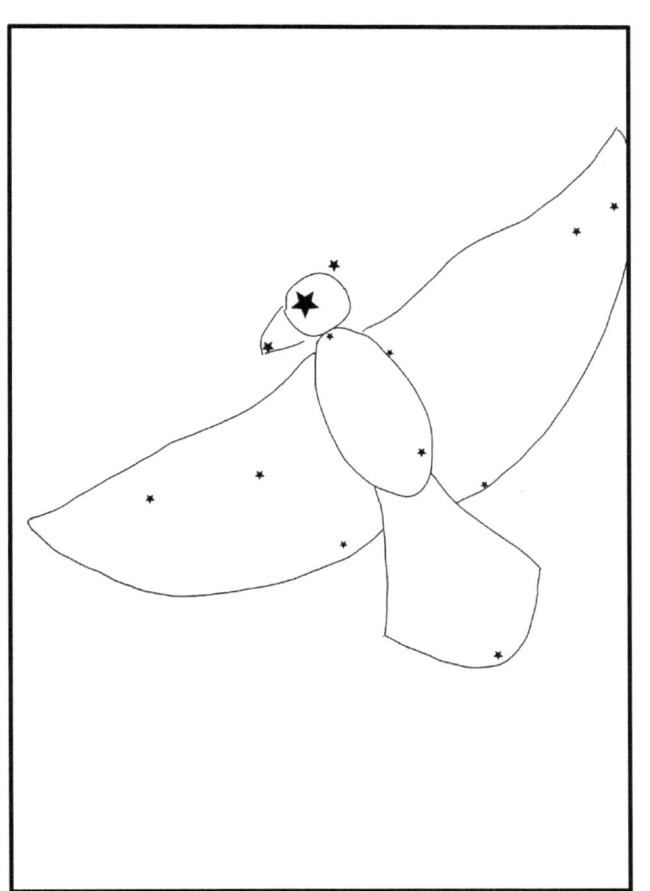

Practice Drawing!

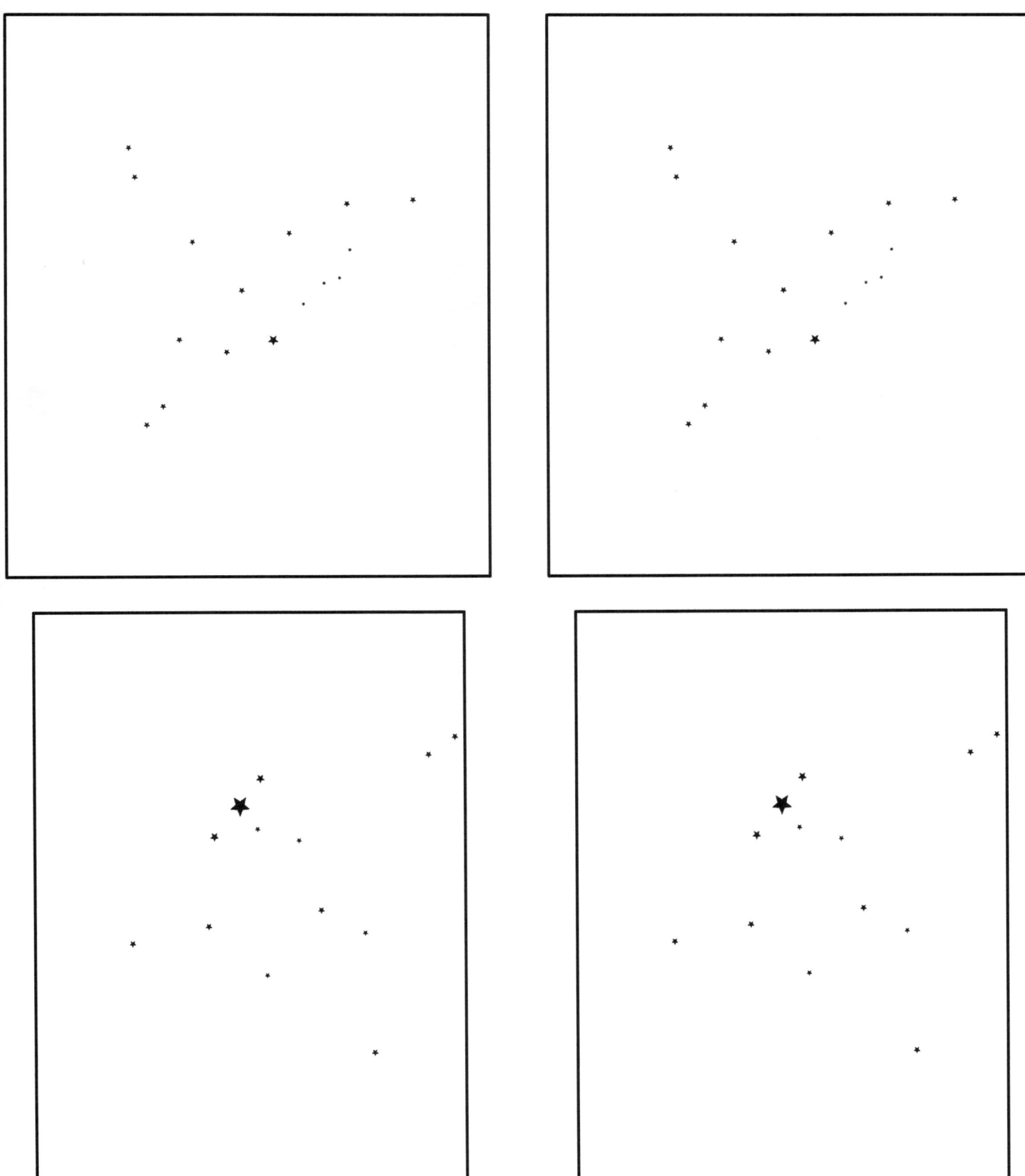

Homework Drawing!

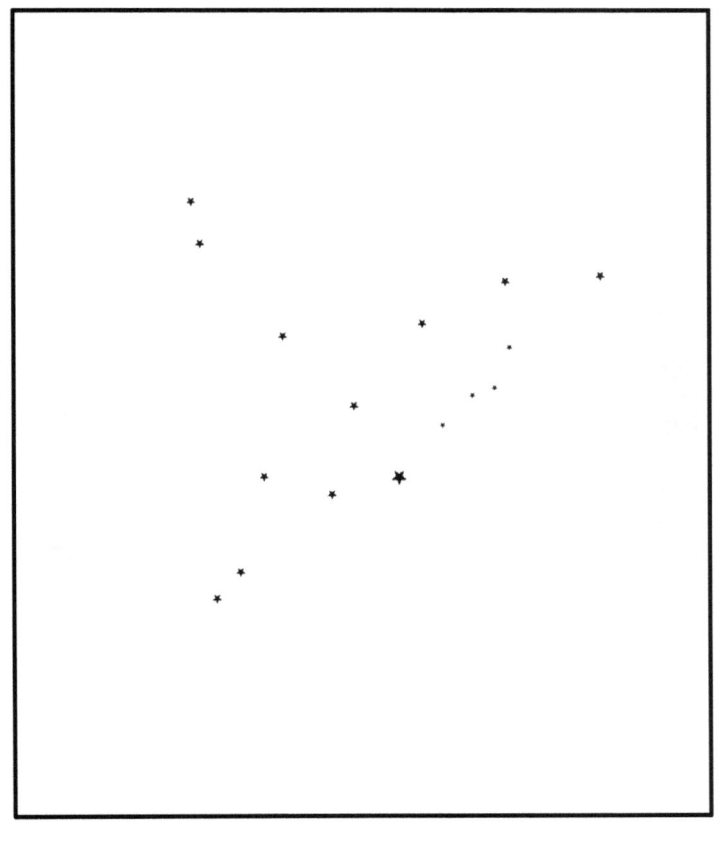

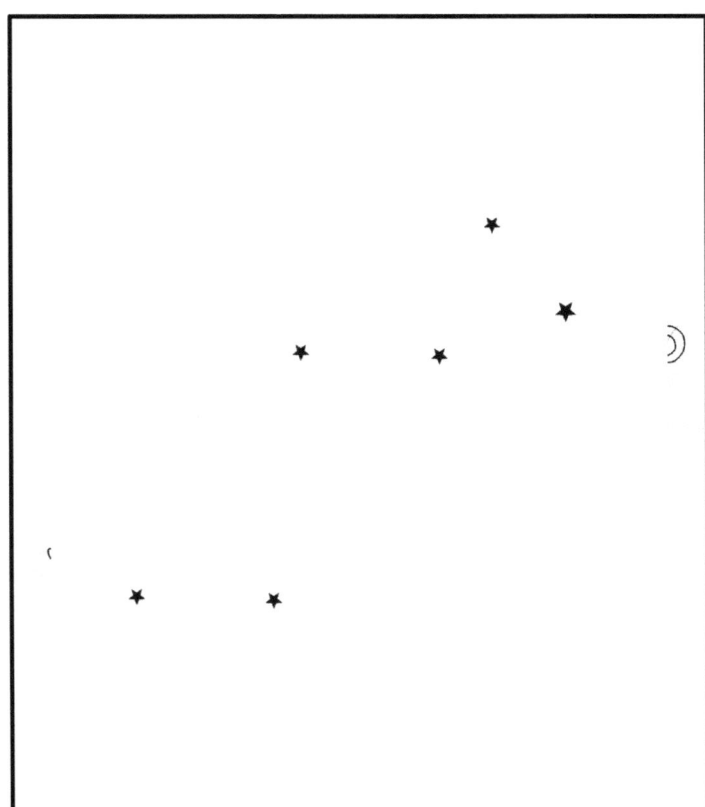

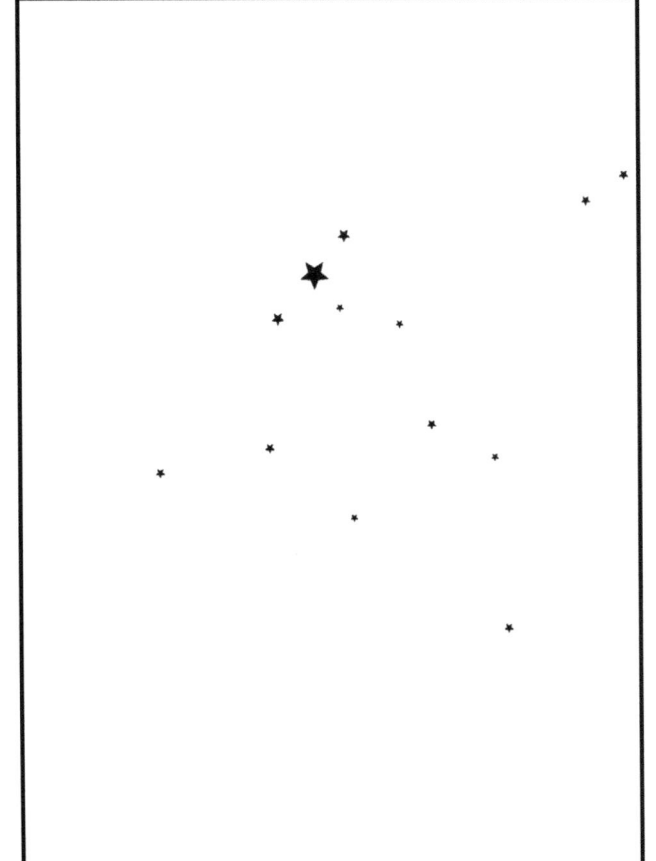

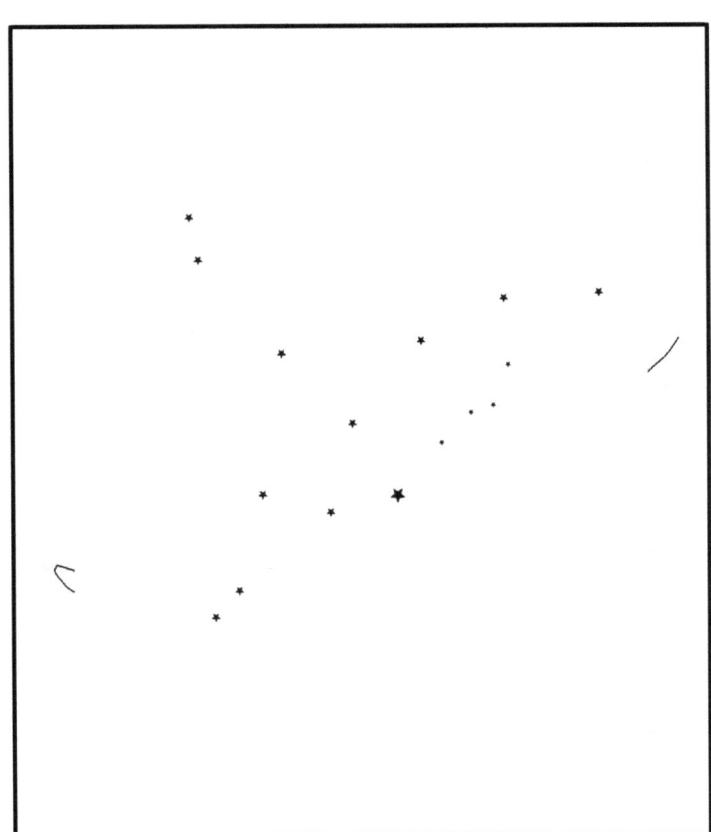

Draco and Hercules

Draco and Hercules

How to Draw Draco

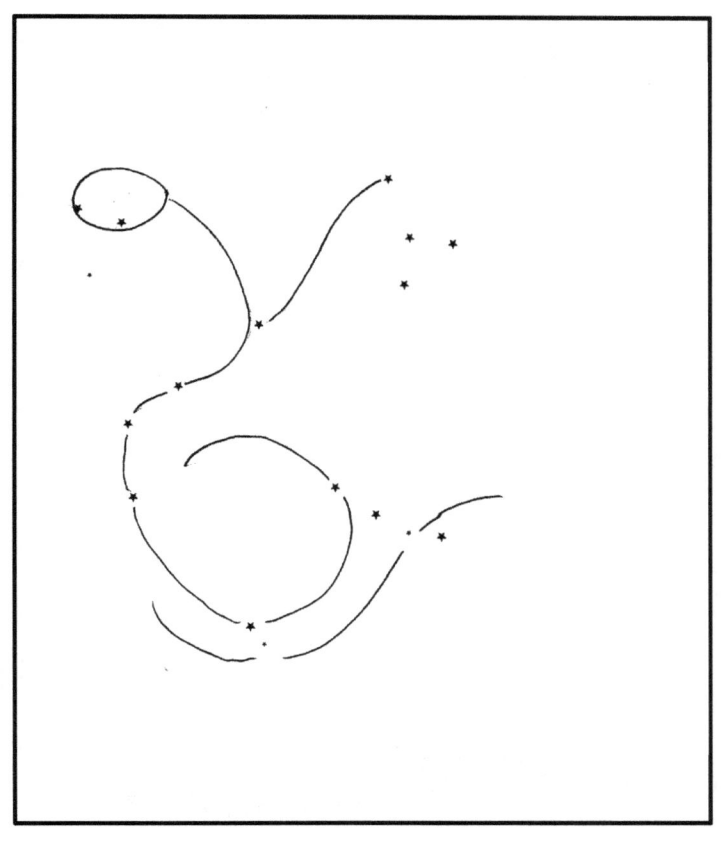

How to Draw Hercules

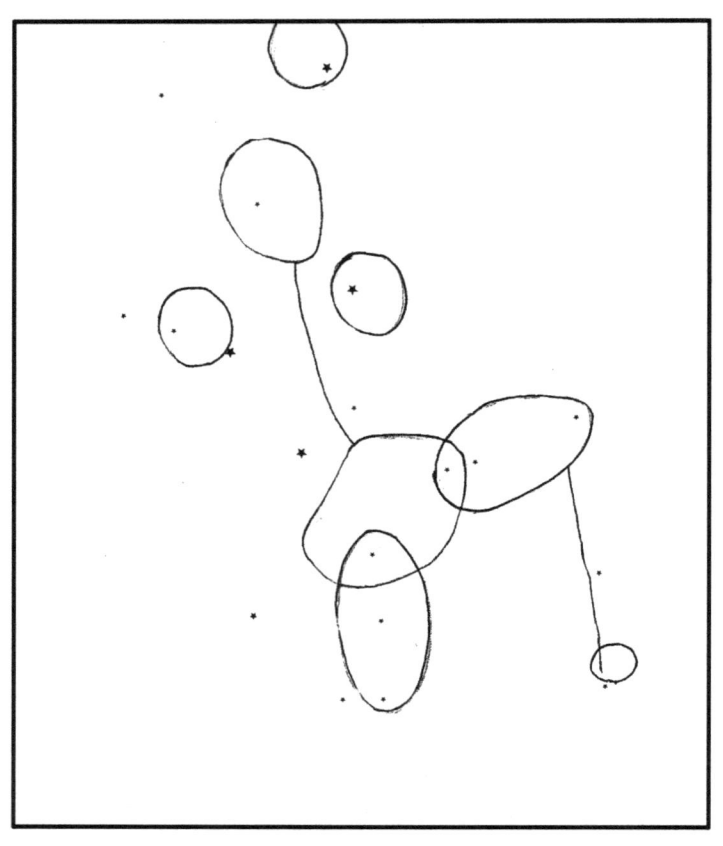

Practice Drawing

Homework Drawing

I was able to see: ☐ Draco ☐ Hercules

Zodiac

Zodiac

How to Draw Scorpio

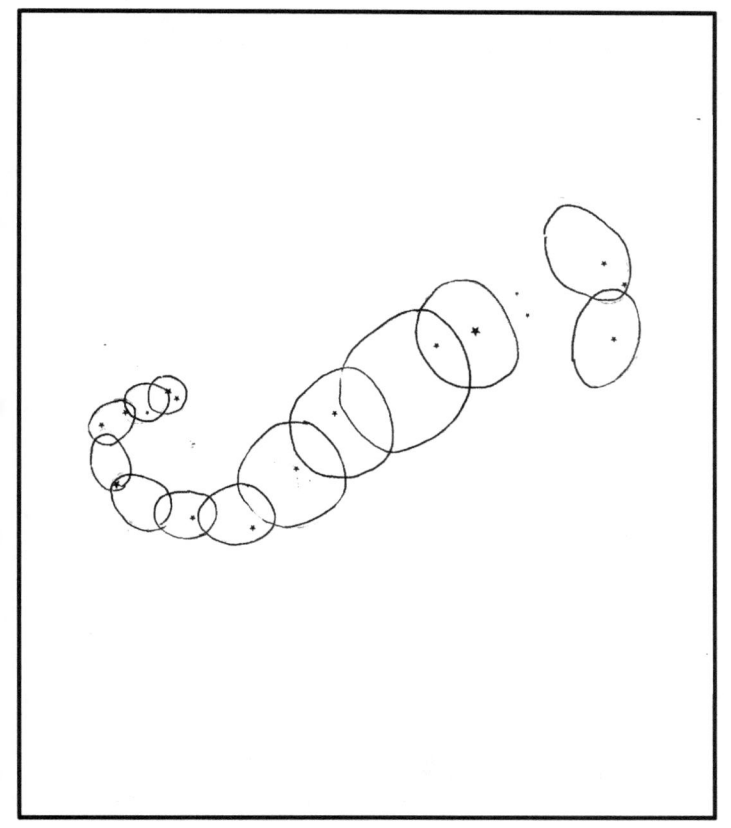

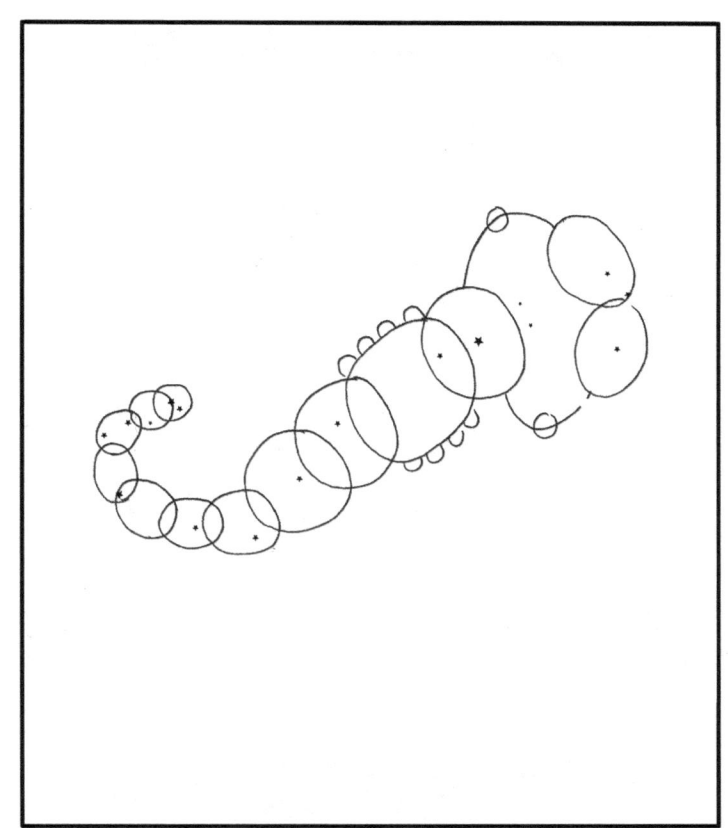

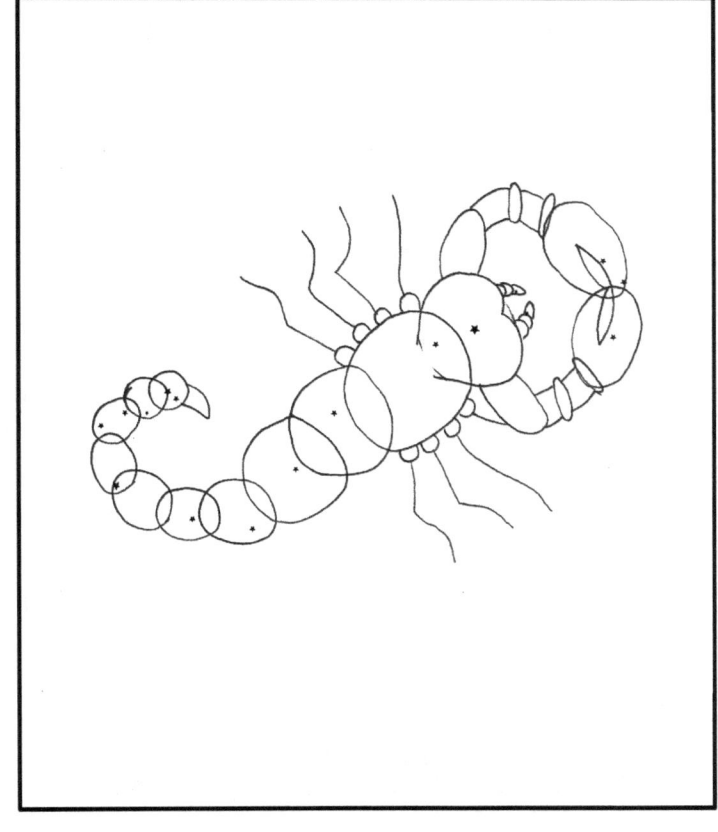

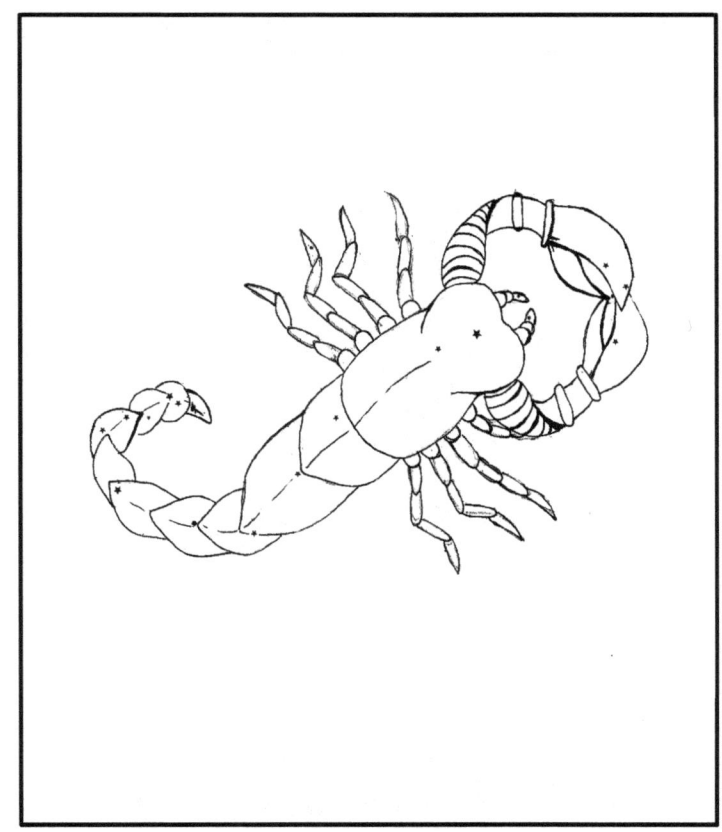

How to Draw Capricornus

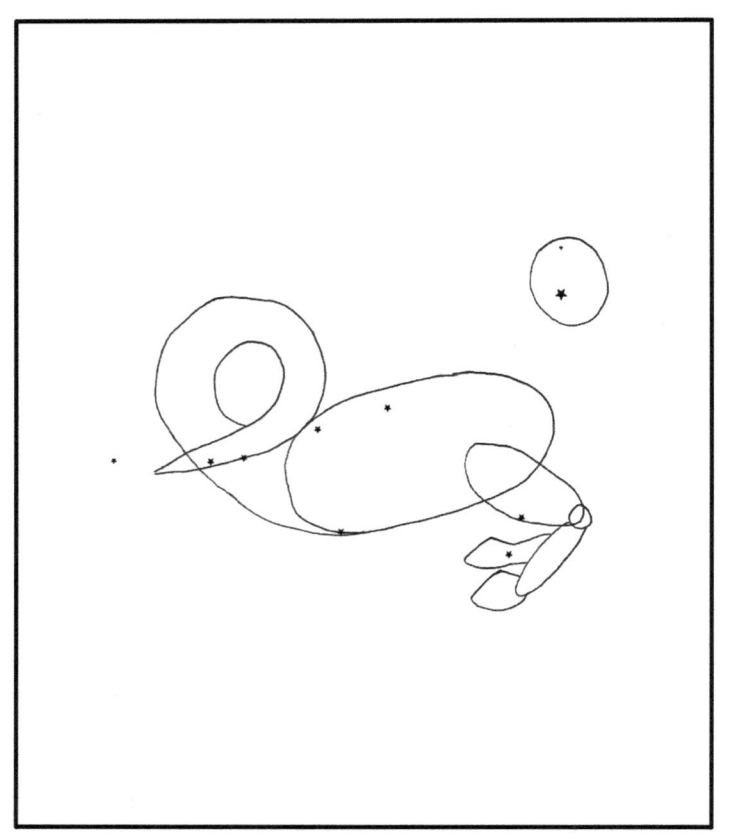

Practice Drawing

Bonus: How to Draw Saggitarius pt.1

This is an extra credit constellation!

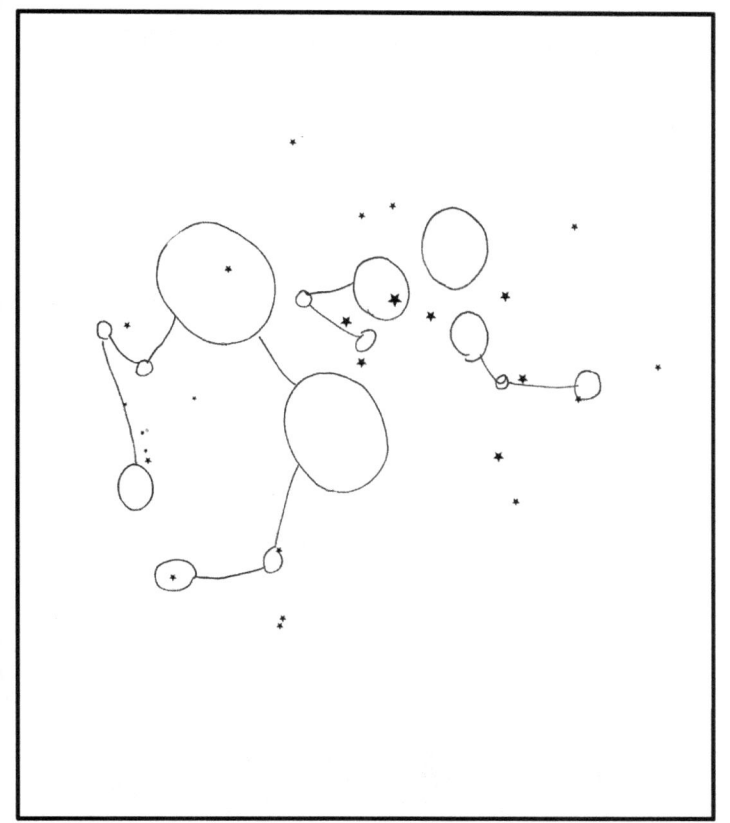
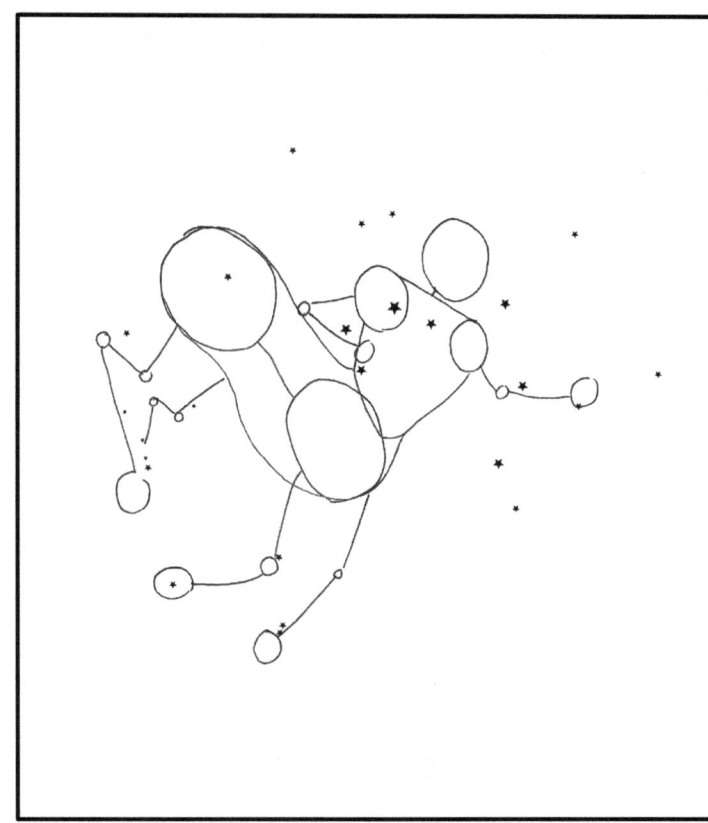

Bonus: How to Draw Saggitarius pt.2

This is an extra credit constellation!

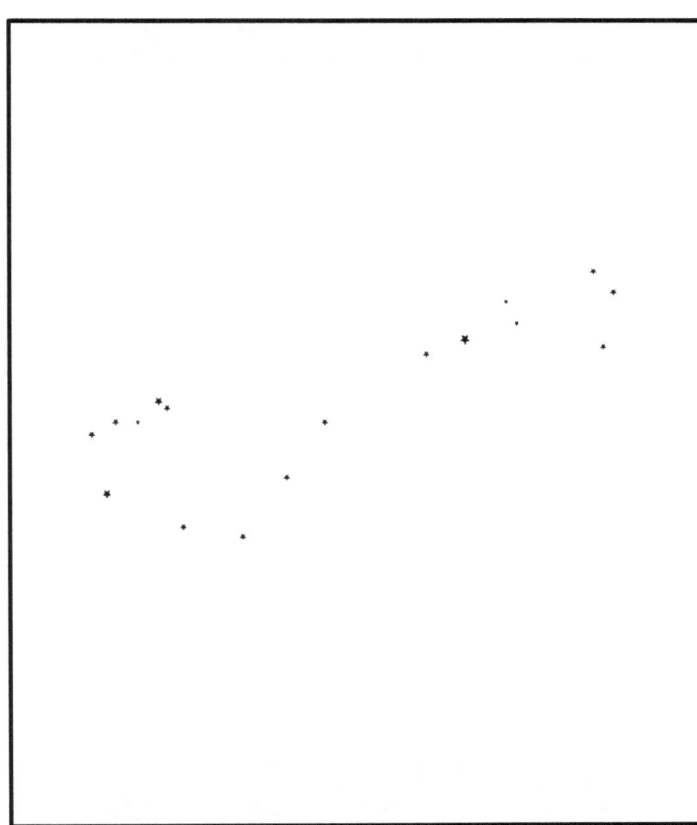

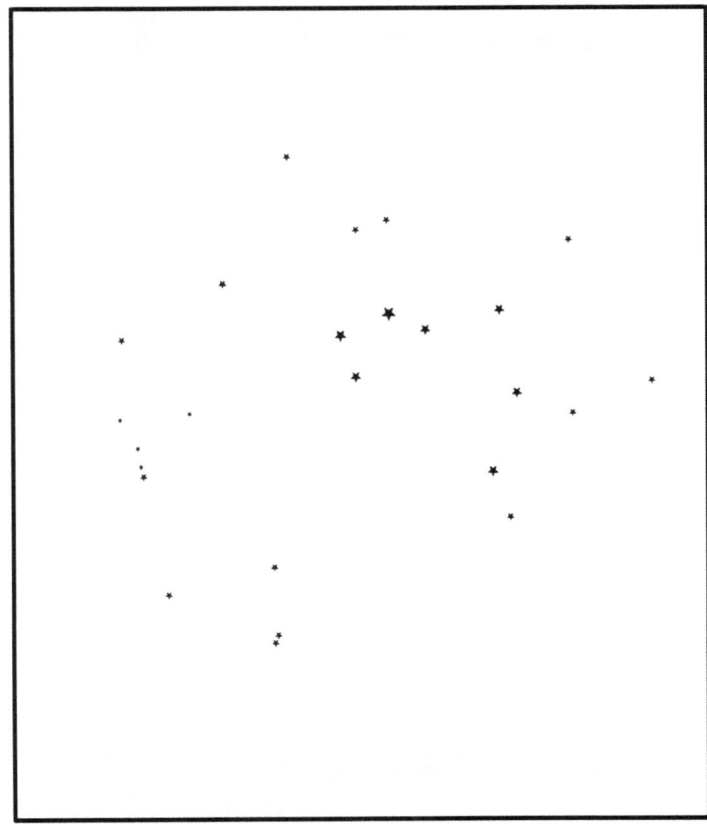

Homework Drawing

I was able to see: ☐ Scorpio ☐ Capricornus ☐ Sagittarius
Make sure to identify the constellations!

Opiuchus, Serpens, Delphinus

Opiuchus, Serpens, Delphinus

How to Draw Opiuchus and Serpens

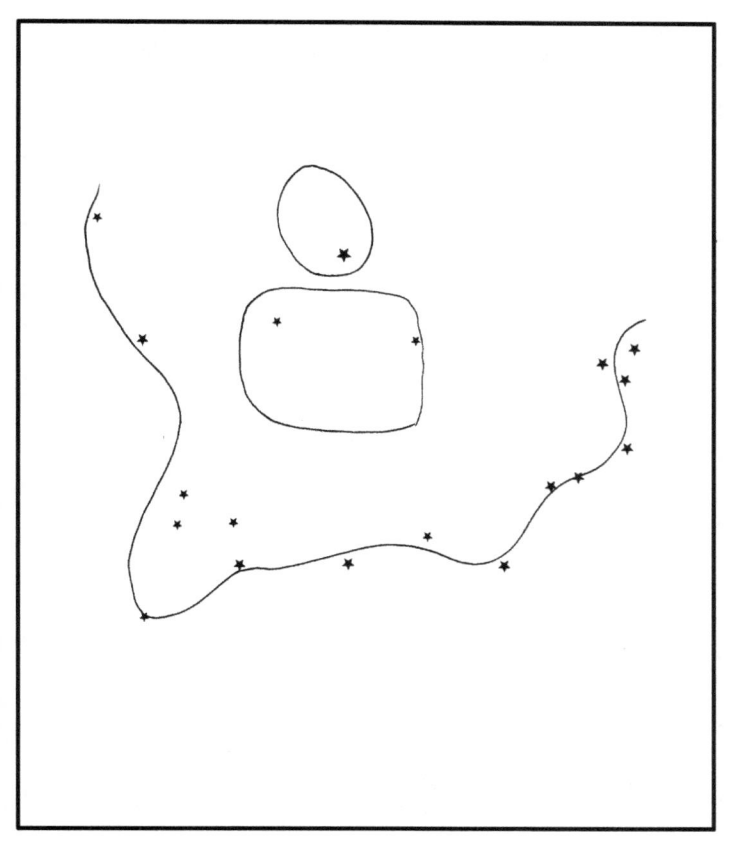
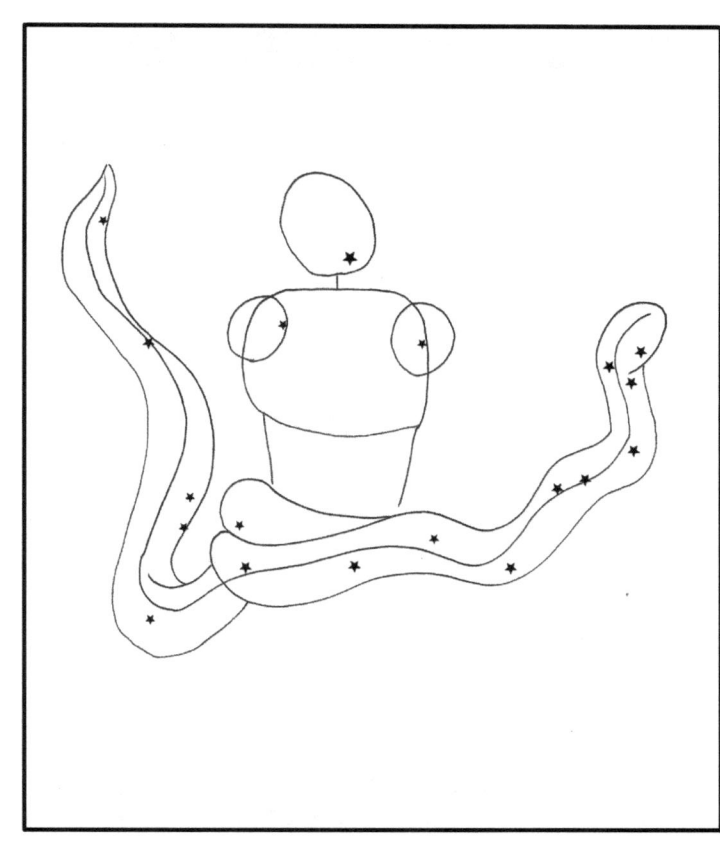
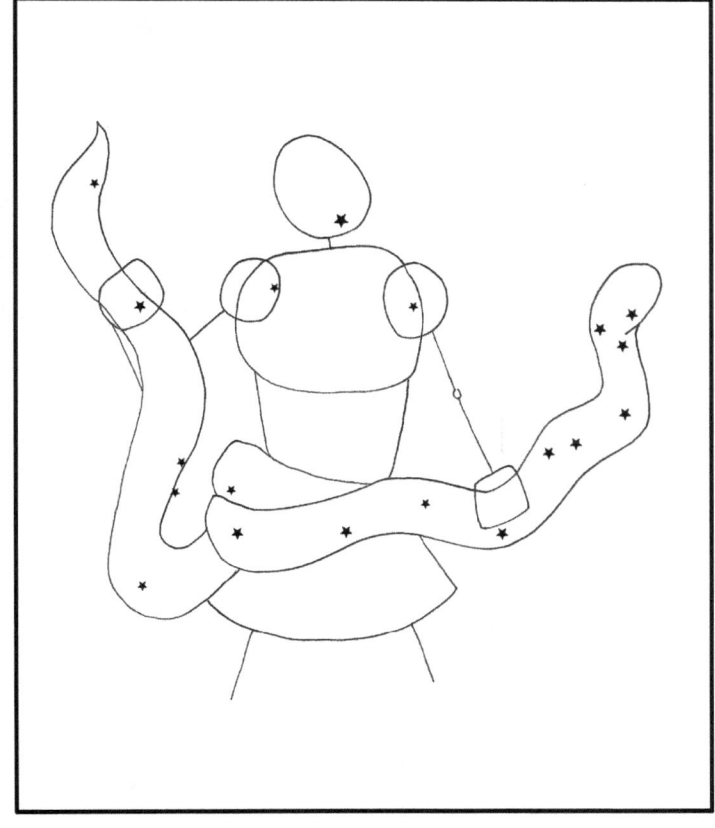

How to Draw Opiuchus, Serpens, and Dolphinus

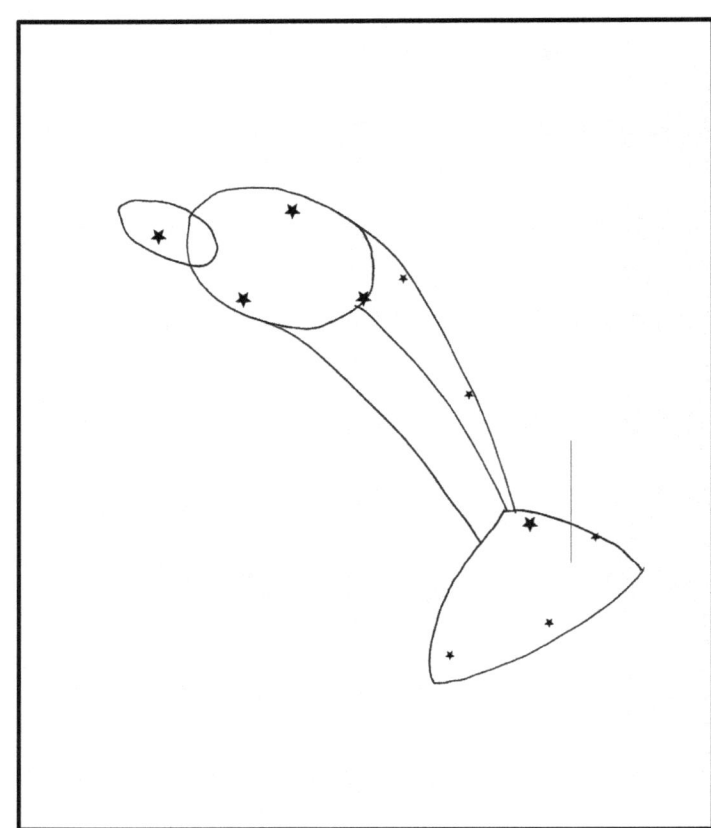

Practice Drawing

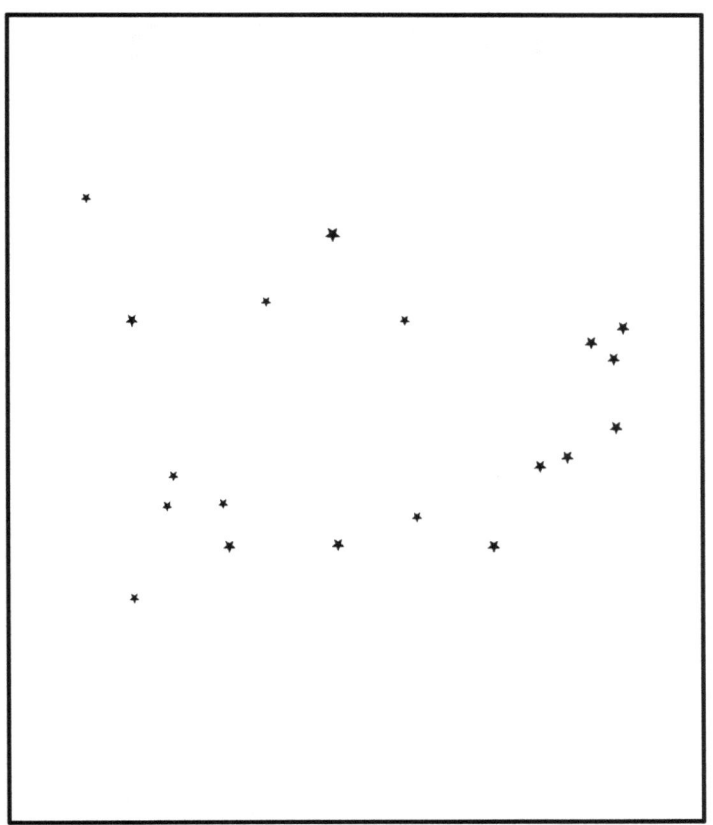

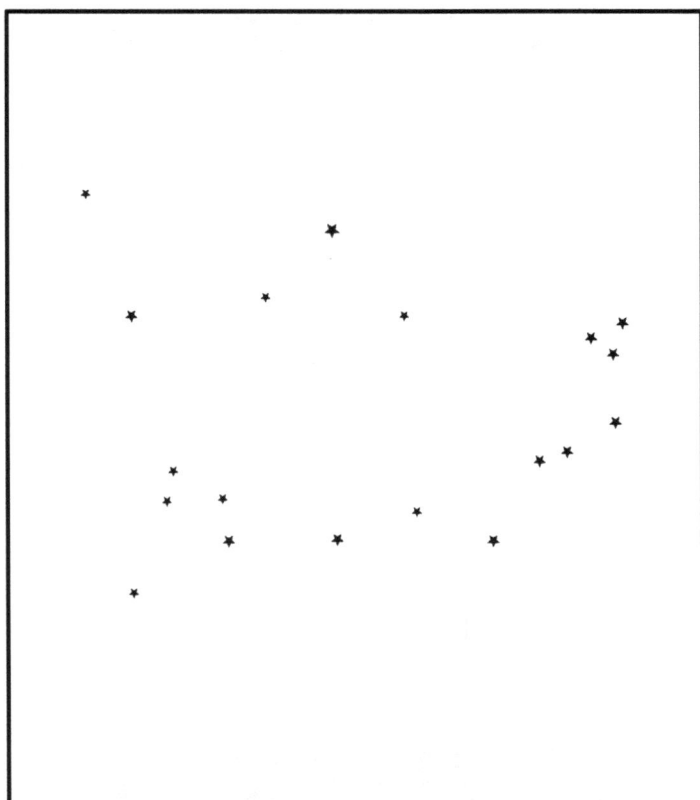

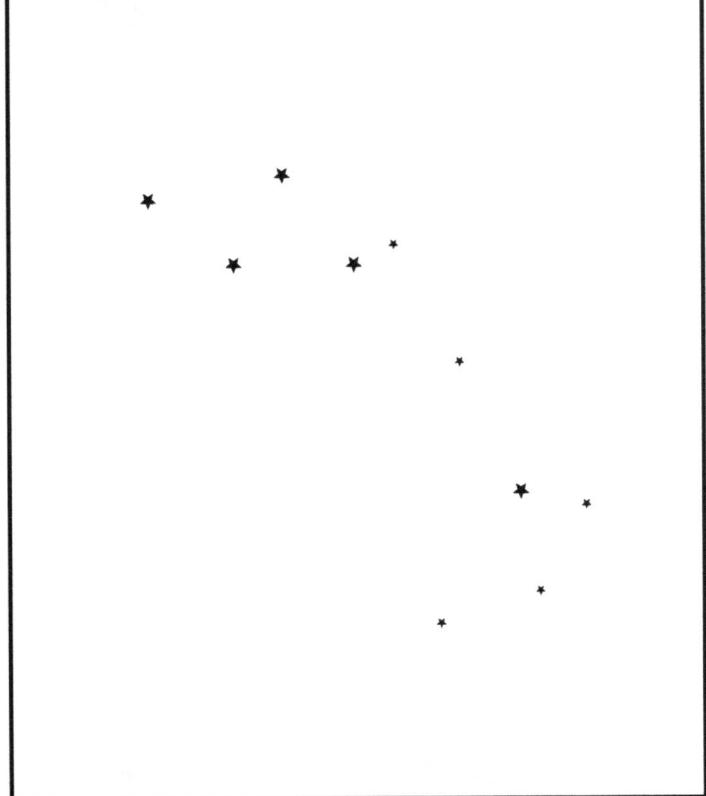

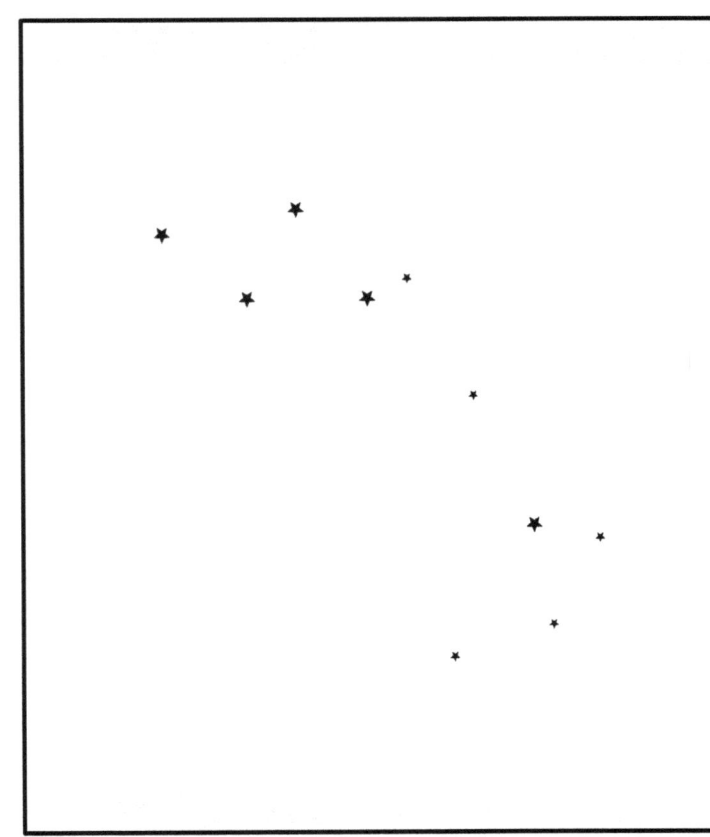

Homework Drawing

I was able to see: ☐ Opiuchus ☐ Serpens   ☐ Dolphinus

Make sure to identify the constellations!

The Sun

The Sun is a great nuclear reactor! The core's temperature is about 27 million degrees F, This is hot enough to continue the constant state of thermonuclear fusion, a process where atoms combine to create larger atoms and in that process they release huge amounts of energy.

It's the energy that is created at the core that acts as the engine that powers the sun and makes all of the light and heat that is emitted from the sun.

The radiation from the photosphere appears as sunlight as it reaches Earth. It takes around 8 minutes from the moment that it leaves the sun to reach our planet.

Every sun has a birth, lifespan and a death. Our sun will continue to shine for around 130 million more years and then it will stop burning its hydrogen and begin to burn helium. When that happens it will expand and grow and eventually engulf Mercury, Venus, and Earth.

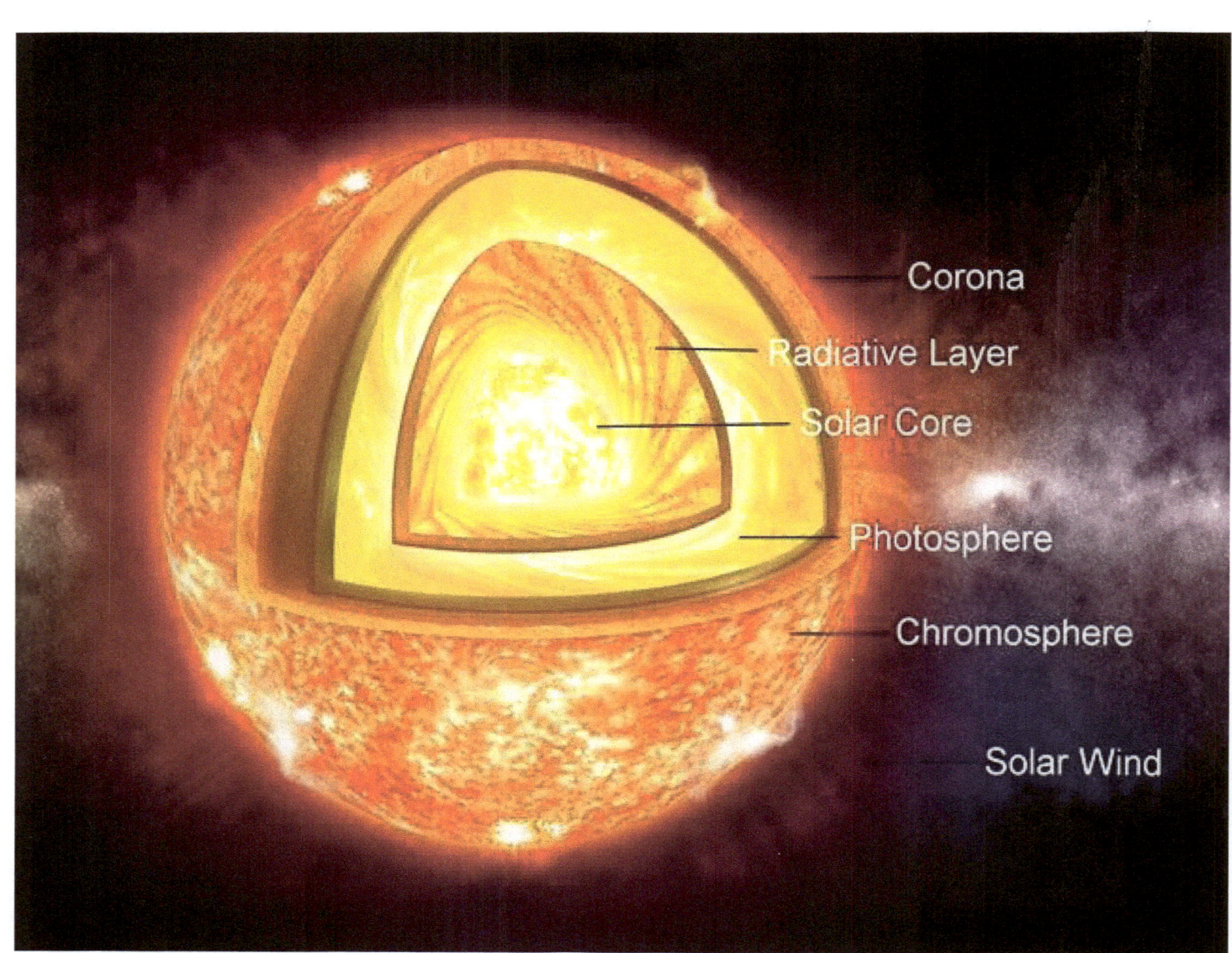

The Earth and Moon

Earth Facts!

She spins around the sun once every **365.25 days** – this is known as one Earth year.

She is around is around 4.5 billion years old!

Layers of the Earth

The Earth's surface is covered by its thinnest layer, the crust. It is mostly made of simple rocks like sandstone and granite.

The Mantle is a solid soft core which is 5432 F in temperature!

The Outer core is made of liquid metal burning at 8832 F! It sloshes around causing a magnetic field.

The Inner core is a solid iron ball, although it is at extreme temperatures (10832 F) it stays solid from the extreme pressure!

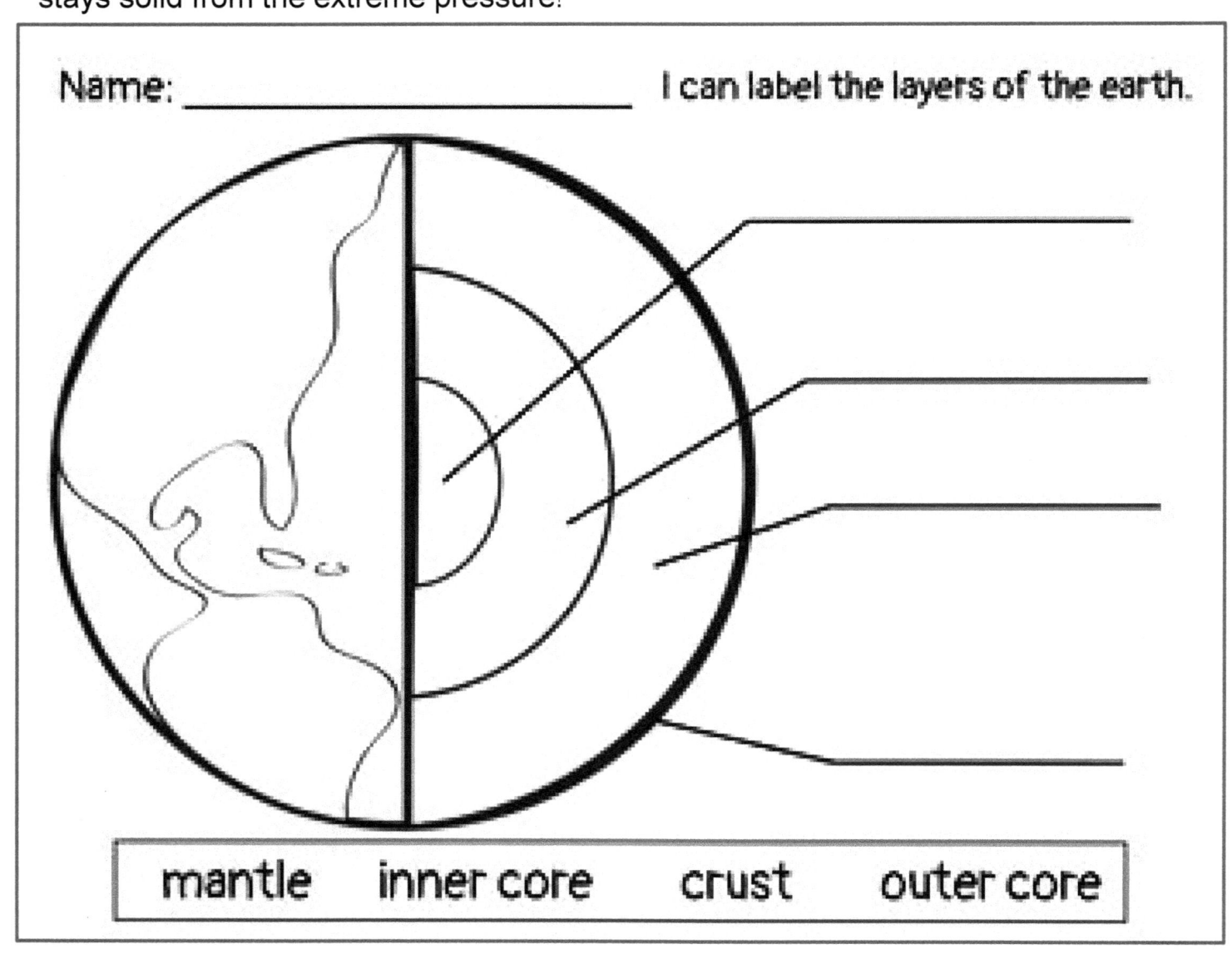

Name: _____   I can label the layers of the earth.

| mantle | inner core | crust | outer core |

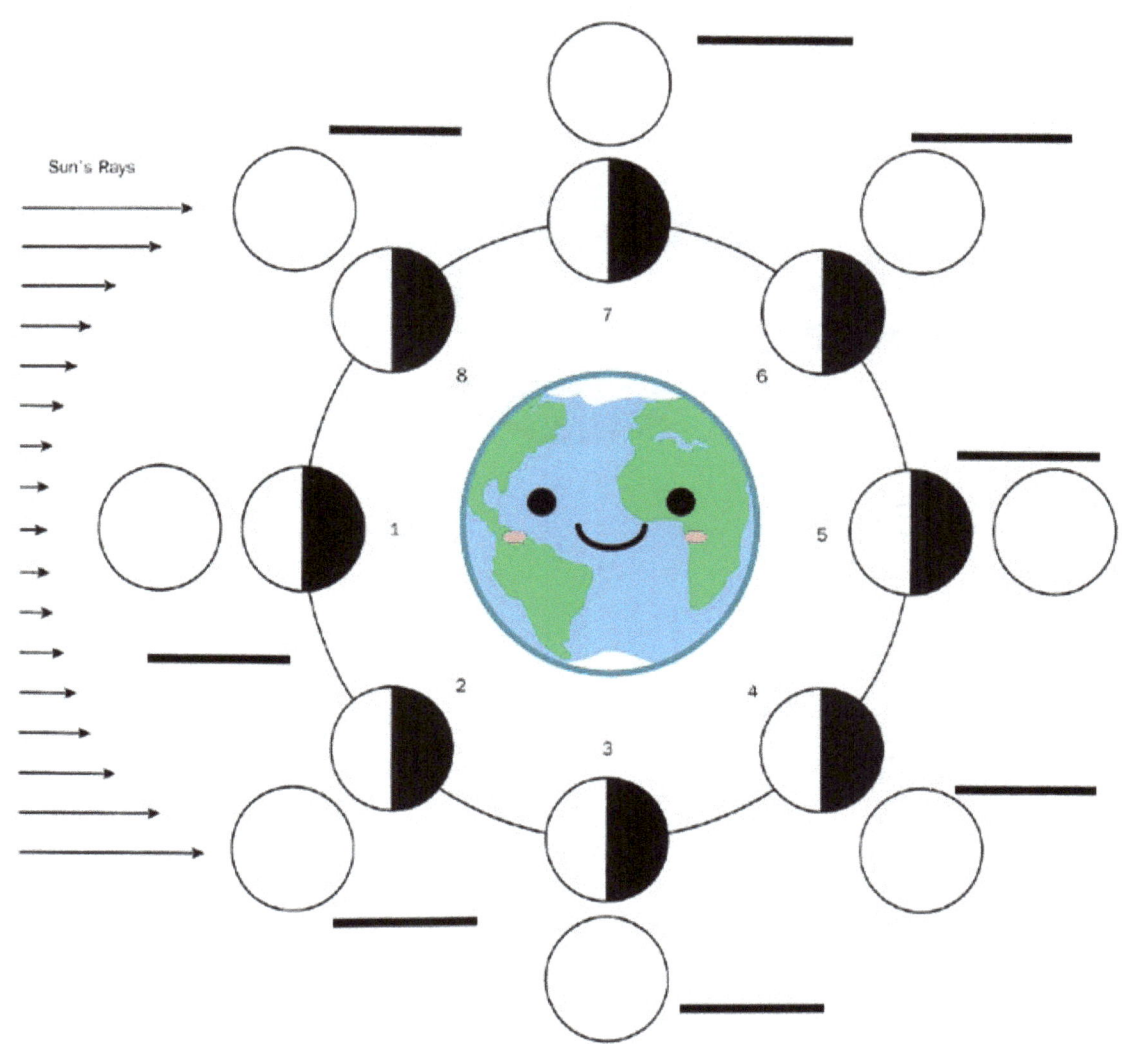

Sun's Rays

Name: _____

Current Moon Phase: _____

Phases of the Earth's Moon

Fill-in the cycle of the moon by naming the remaining major 7 phases, and correctly shading the shape. Make sure your shading and names match.

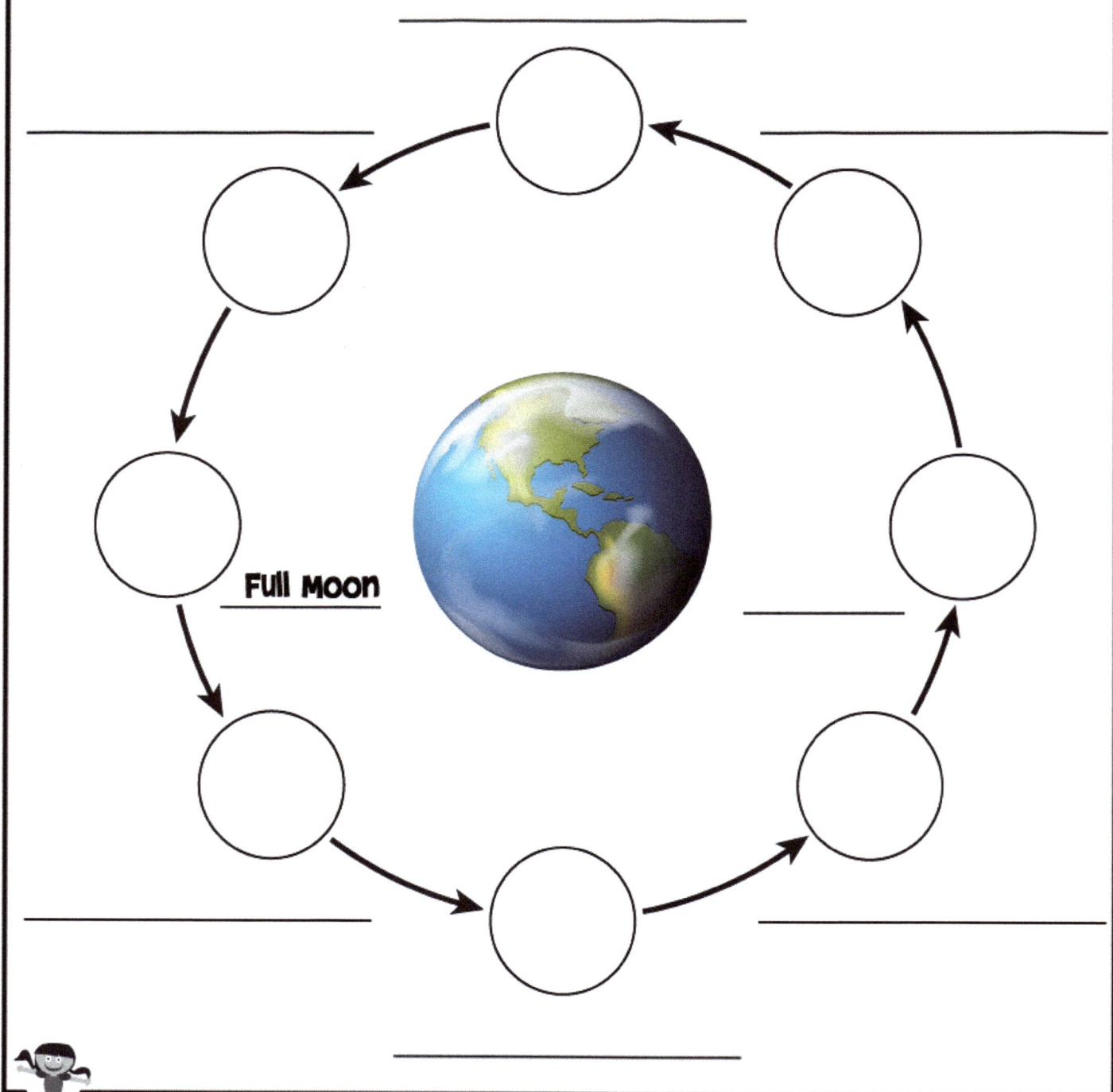

_____

_____

Full Moon _____

_____

_____

_____

Andromeda was the daughter of the weak King Cepheus of Ethiopia and the vain Queen Cassiopeia, whose boastfulness knew no bounds.

The princess's misfortunes began one day when her mother claimed that she was more beautiful even than the Nereids, a particularly alluring group of sea nymphs. The affronted Nereids decided that Cassiopeia's vanity had finally gone too far and they asked Poseidon, the sea god, to teach her a lesson. In retribution, Poseidon sent a terrible monster to ravage the coasts. Dismayed at the destruction, and with his subjects clamouring for action, the beleaguered Cepheus appealed to the Oracle for a solution. He was told that he must sacrifice his daughter to appease the monster.

This is why blameless Andromeda came to be chained to a rock to atone for the sins of her mother, who watched from the shore with bitter remorse. As Andromeda stood on the wave-lashed cliffs, pale with terror and weeping pitifully at her impending fate, the hero Perseus, who we talked about before, happened by, fresh from his exploit of beheading Medusa the Gorgon. His heart was captivated by the sight of the frail beauty in distress below.

Perseus at first almost mistook her for a marble statue. Only the wind ruffling her hair and the warm tears on her cheeks showed that she was human. Perseus asked her name and why she was chained there. Shy Andromeda, totally different in character from her vainglorious mother, did not at first reply; even though awaiting a horrible death in the monster's slavering jaws, she would have hidden her face modestly in her hands, had they not been bound to the rock.

Perseus persisted in his questioning. Eventually, afraid that her silence might be misinterpreted as guilt, she told Perseus her story, but broke off with a scream as she saw the monster breasting through the waves towards her. Perseus swooped down, slew the sea-dragon with his diamond sword, released the girl to the enthusiastic applause of the onlookers and asked to marry her.. Andromeda later bore Perseus six children including Perses, ancestor of the Persians, and Gorgophonte, father of Tyndareus, king of Sparta.

After she grew old and died, the Greek goddess Athene placed Andromeda's image among the stars, where she lies between Perseus and her mother Cassiopeia. Posiodian, still mad that Andromeda escaped placed next to her the sea monster, Cetus.

Andromeda, Cassiopeia, Cephus

Andromeda, Cassiopeia, Cephus

How to Draw

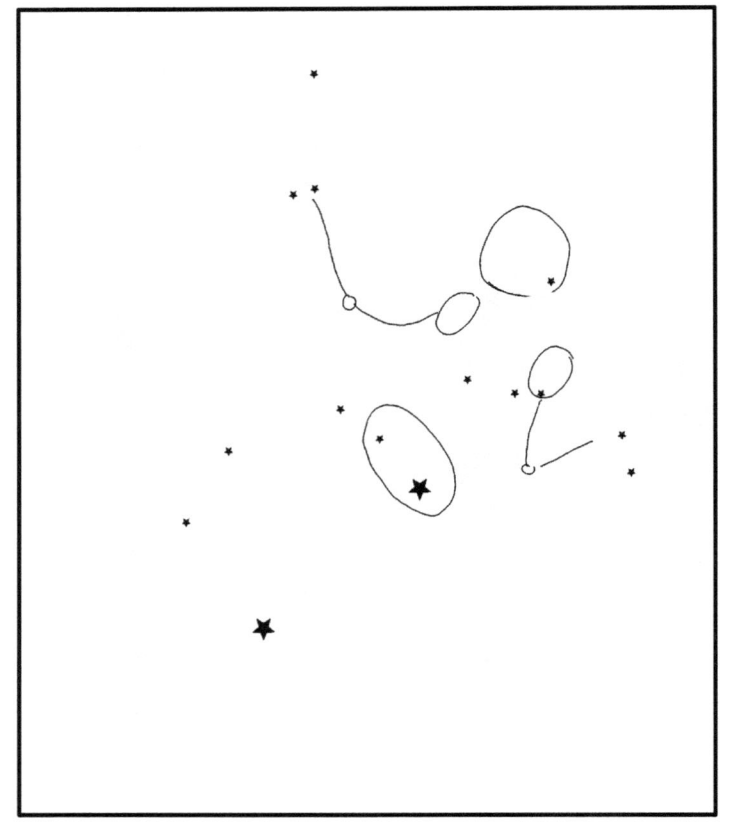
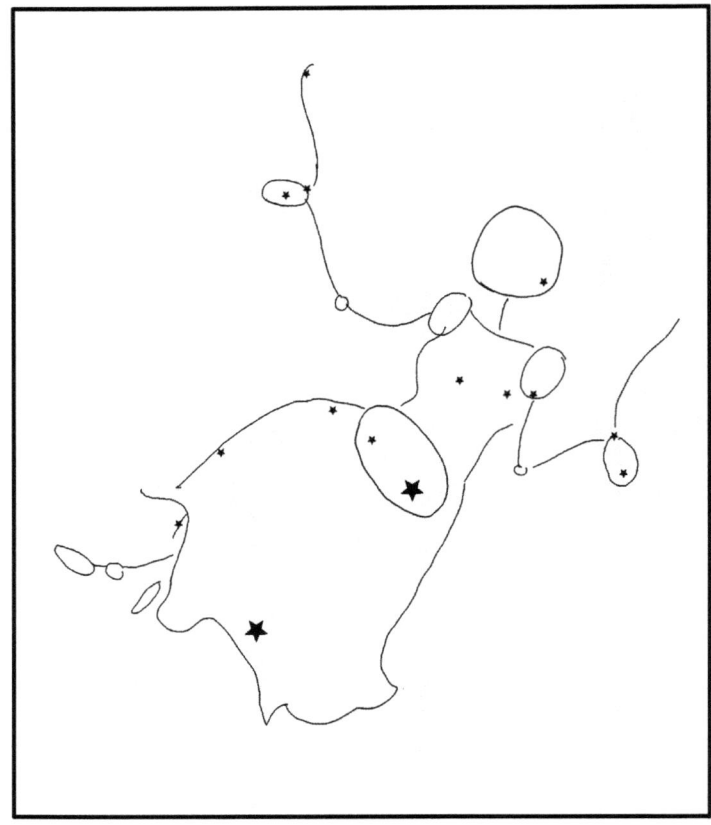
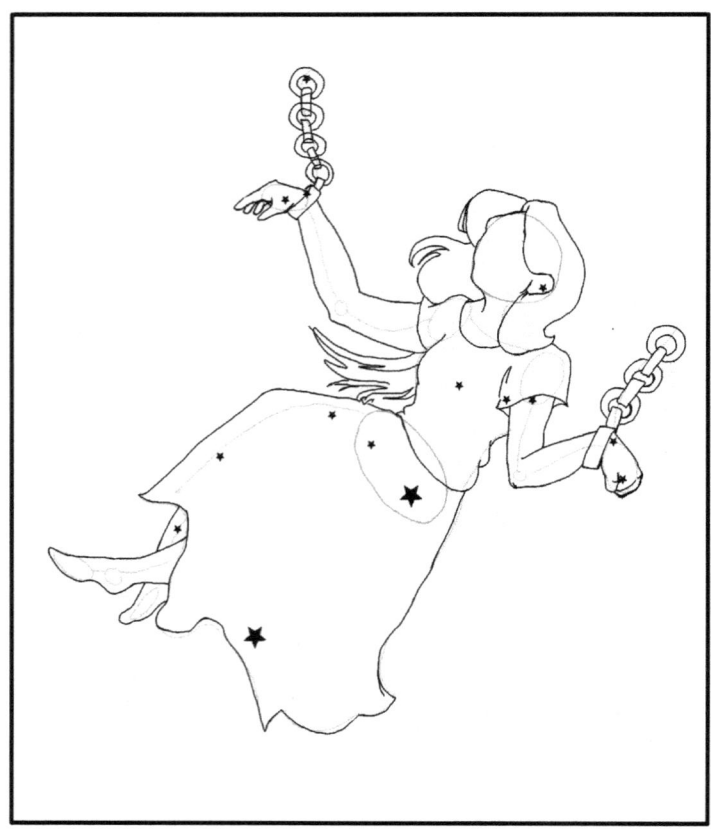

How to Draw

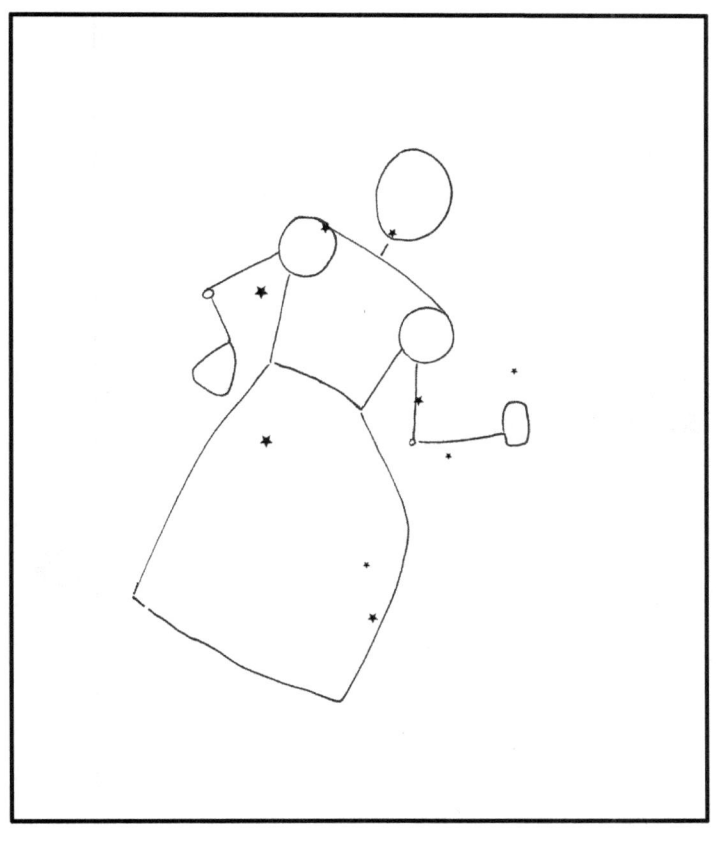

How to Draw

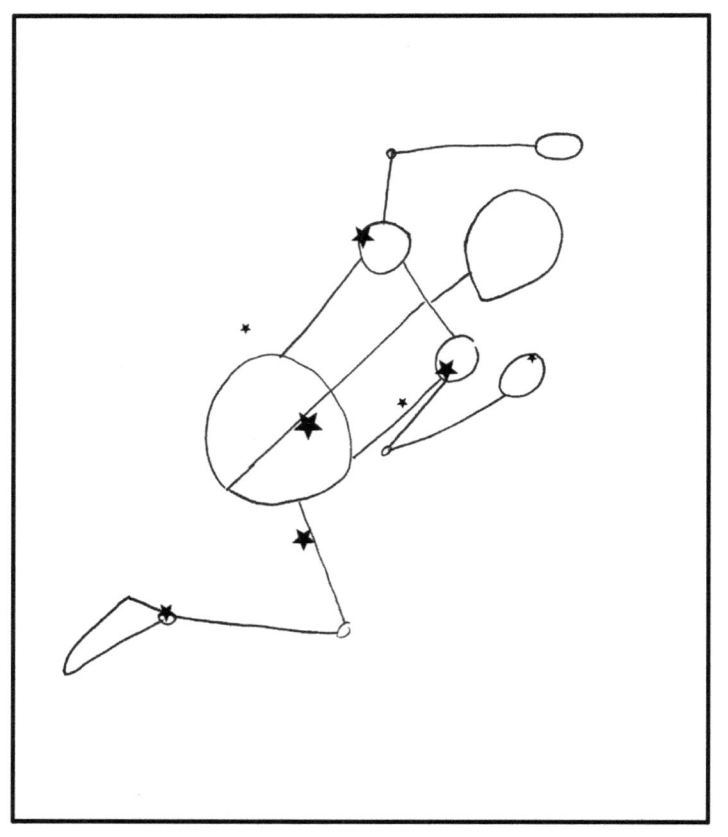
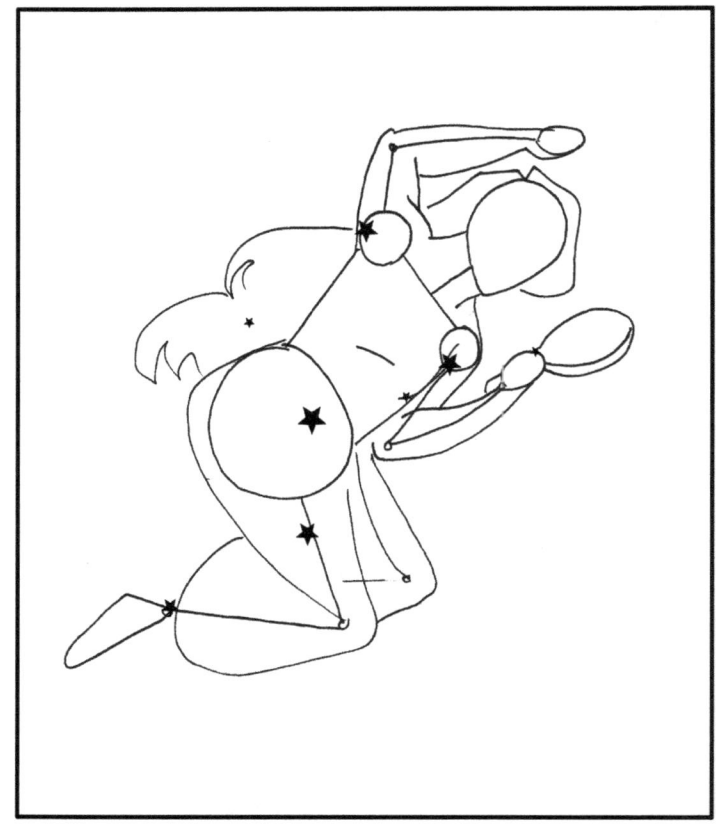

Practice Drawing

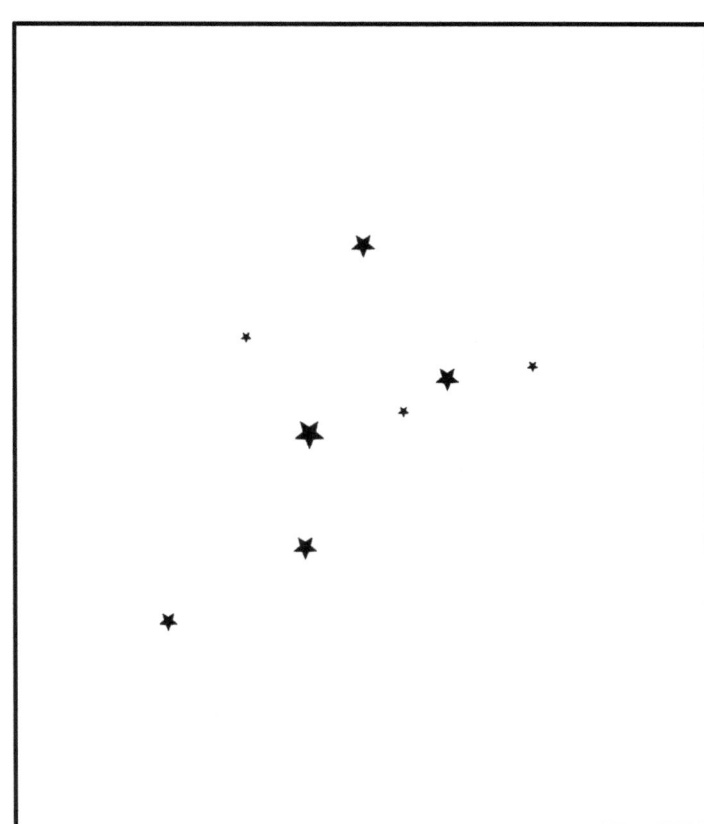

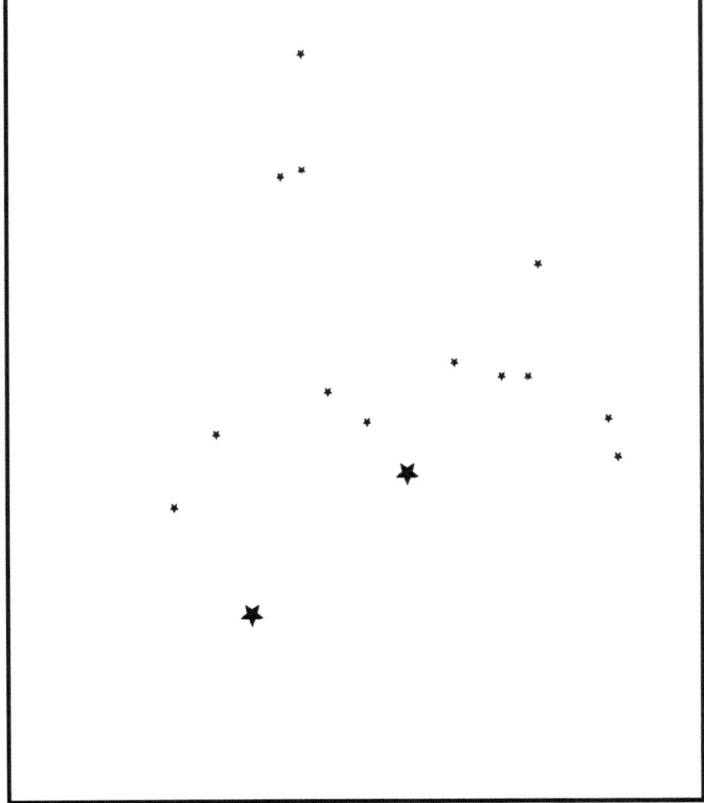

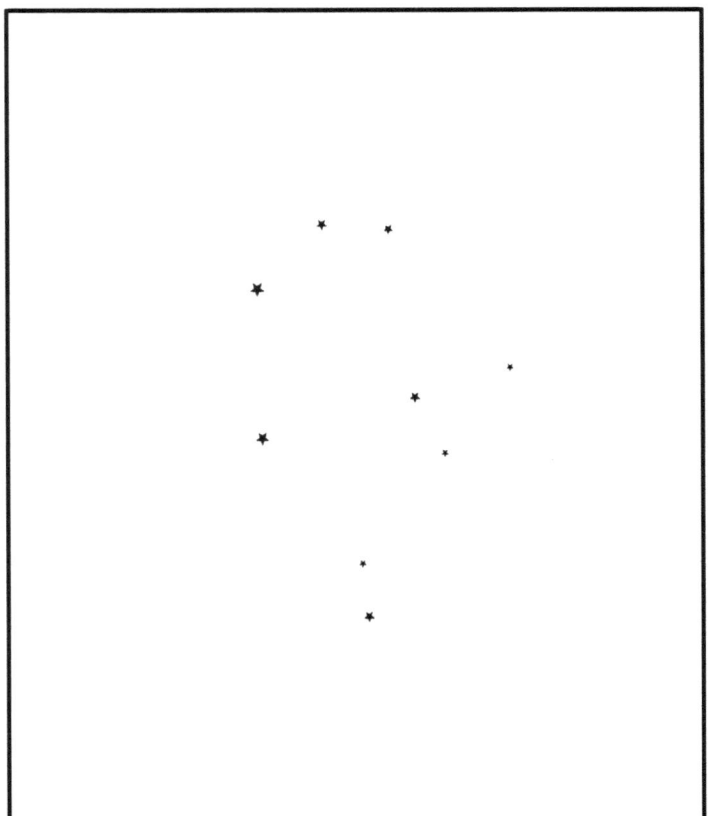

Homework Drawing

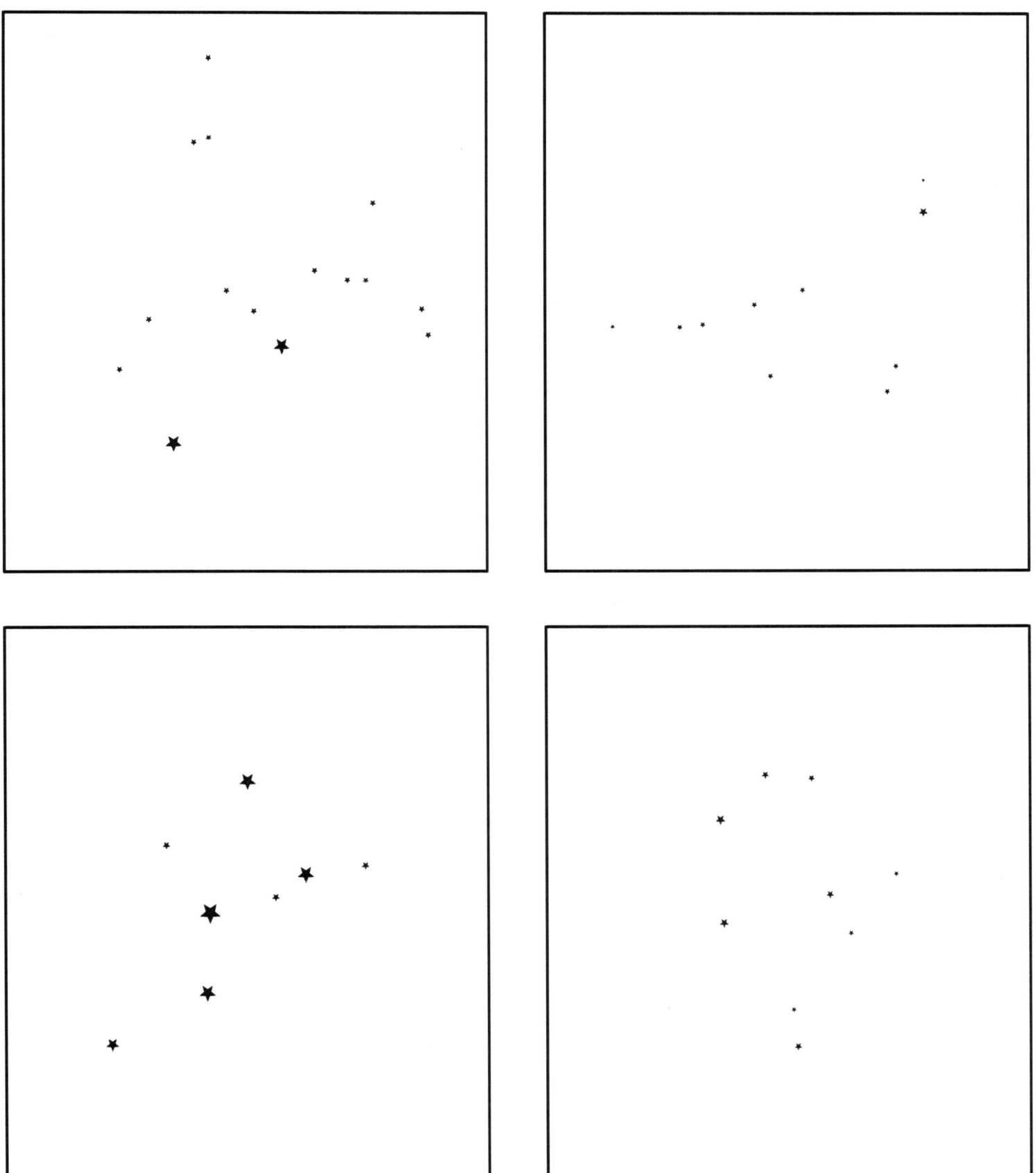

Zodiac pt.2

Zodiac pt.2

How to Draw Aries

How to Draw Pisces

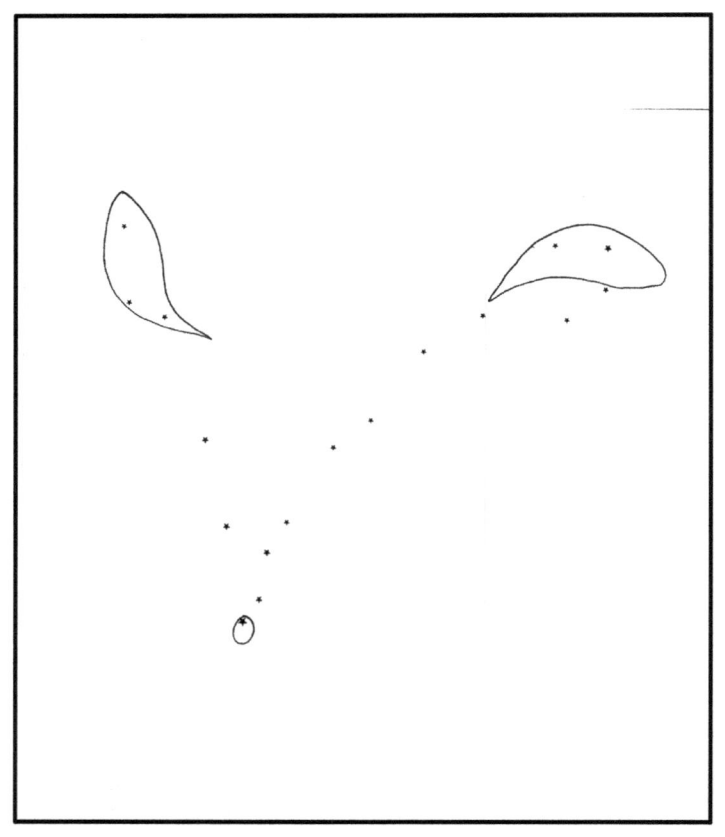
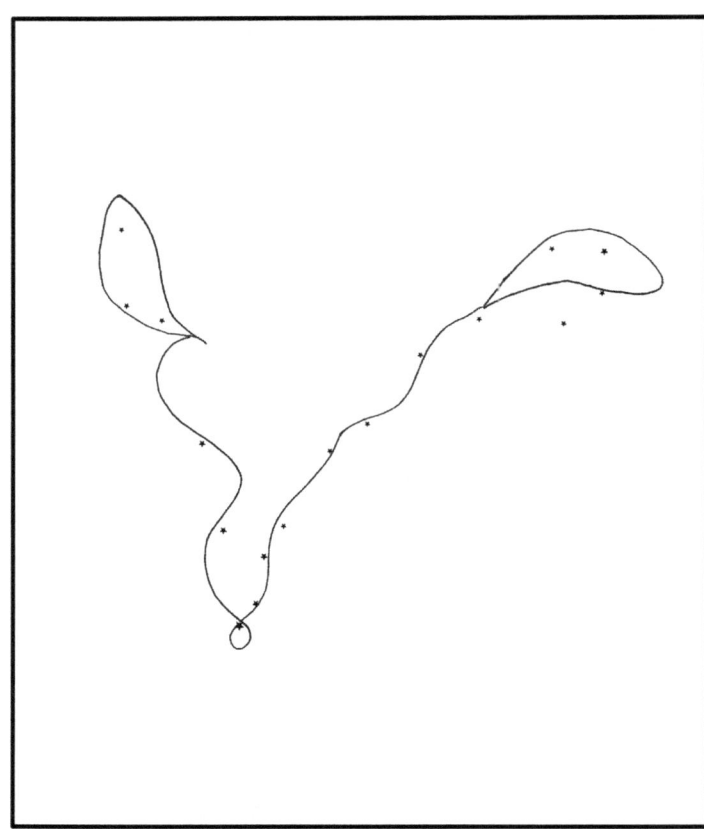
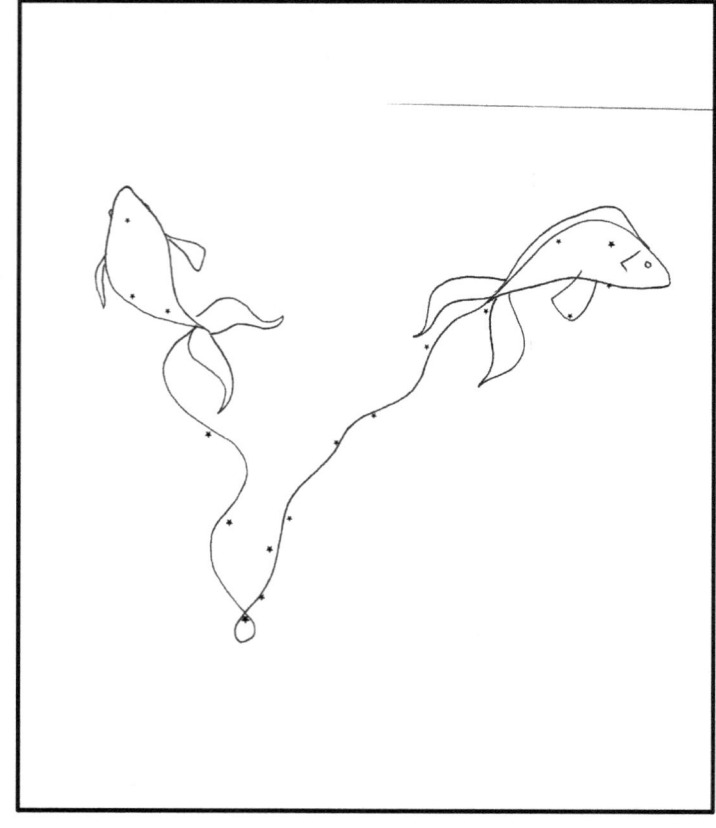
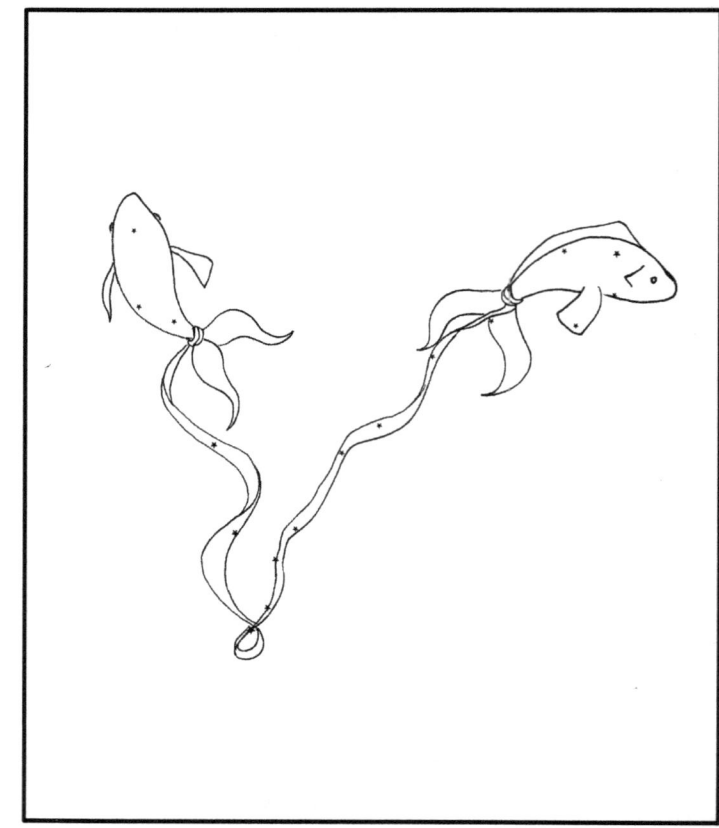

How to Draw Aquilla

Practice Drawing

Homework Drawing

I was able to see: ☐ Pisces   ☐ Aries   ☐ Aquarius
Make sure to identify the constellations!

Mercury

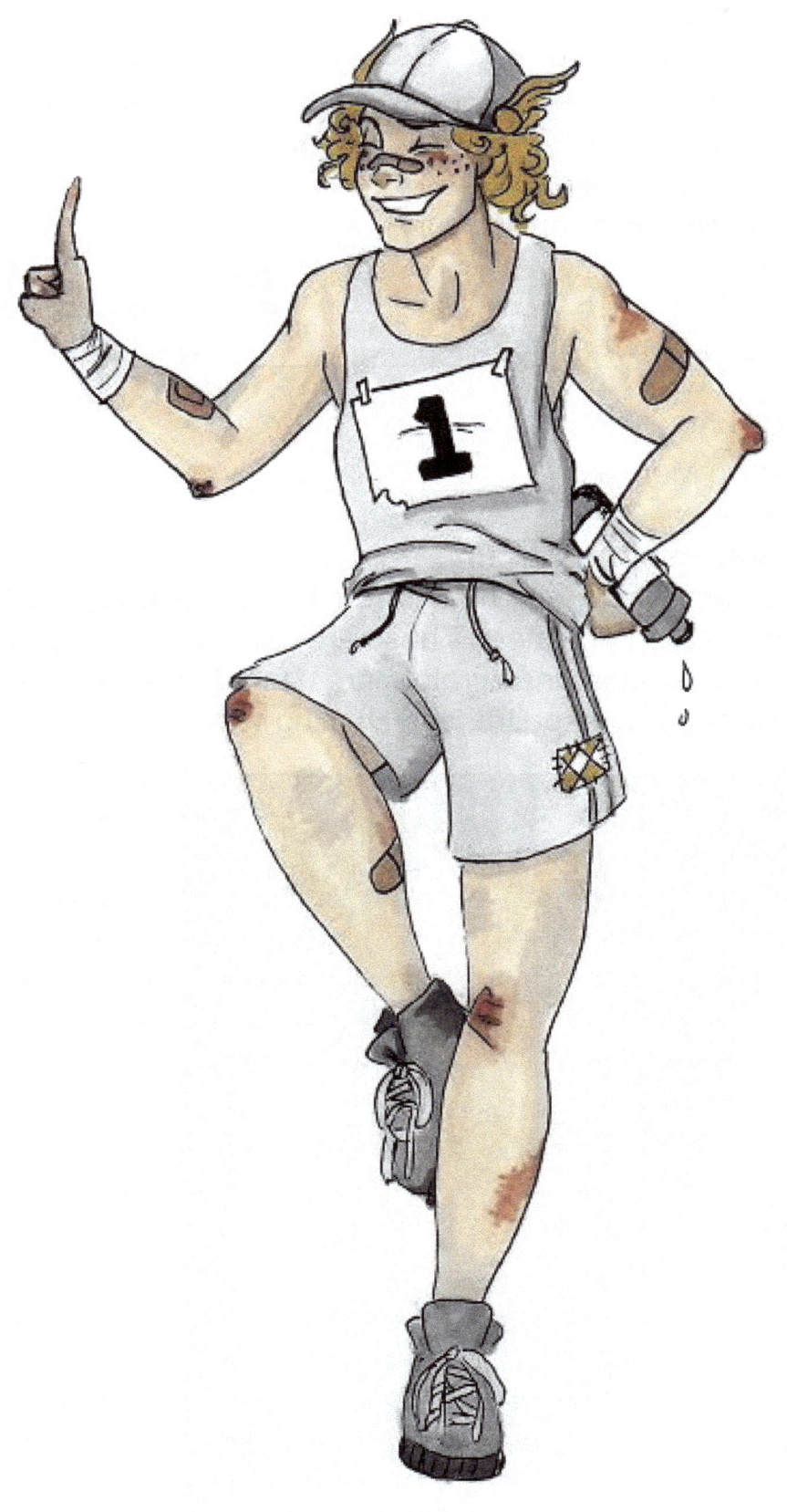

Mercury is the _____ planet in line from the Sun.

Mercury has _____ moons.

What is the average temperature on Mercury? _____

How long is one day on Mercury? _____

How long is one year on Mercury? _____

Other interesting things about Mercury:
Unlike many other planets which "self-heal" through natural geological processes, the surface of Mercury is covered in craters. These are caused by numerous encounters with asteroids and comets. Most Mercurian craters are named after famous writers and artists, including Back, Lovecraft, Shakespeare, and Hemingway.

There is a little water on Mercury, but it is constantly evaporating by the solar winds.

Venus

Venus is the _____ planet in line from the Sun.

Venus has _____ moons.

What is the average temperature on Venus? _____

How long is one day on Venus? _____

How long is one year on Venus? _____

Other interesting things about Venus:
Venus rotates in the opposite direction to most other planets. This means that Venus is rotating in the opposite direction to the Sun, this is also known as a retrograde rotation. One possible reason for this might be a collision with an asteroid or other object.

Venus has an incredibly thick coat of clouds. These clouds trap tons of heat on the planet They also reflect a lot of light, Venus is the second brightest object in the night sky, only th moon is brighter!

Venus is known as Earth's "Twin Sister" as they are about the same size. People used to think that Venu was a tropical paradise, but once we sent satellites out there we found it to be inhospitable because of the high heat and sulpher content.

Mars

Mars is the _____ planet in line from the Sun.

Mars has _____ moons.

What is the average temperature on Mars? _____

How long is one day on Mars? _____

How long is one year on Mars? _____

Other interesting things about Mars:
Mars has a red colour because its surface is mostly made of Iron dust! This iron gets rusty and that causes the red martian colour.
Mars also has ice caps! Not only that it has tons of riverbeds, and dark stains that indicate trickling water. Most of the water is gone because it has very little atmosphere. Why? Because Mars has a broken magnetic shield! It does not protect from the solar wind anymore so its atmosphere has blown away. Many scientists believe that Mars used to have life, but after the shield broke the Sun's solar radiation killed all life on mars, blew away the atmosphere, causing it to turn much colder!

Mars has two moons, Phobos and Deimos, and they are small and lumpy.

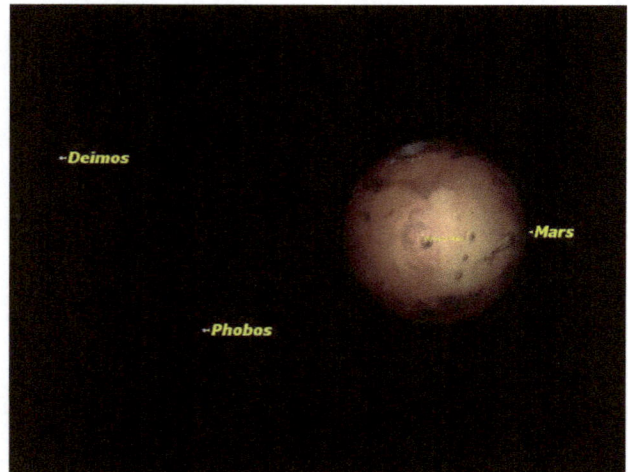

Name: _____

Date: _____

Planet: _____

Fact 1:
_____
_____

Fact 2:
_____
_____

Planet: _____

Fact 1:
_____
_____

Fact 2:
_____
_____

Planet: _____

Fact 1:
_____
_____

Fact 2:
_____
_____

Planet: _____

Fact 1:
_____
_____

Fact 2:
_____
_____

Object: _____

What is this?
_____
_____
_____

Object: _____

What is this?
_____
_____
_____

Group of Objects: _____

What is this?
_____
_____
_____

Perseus, Pegasus, and Cetus

Perseus, Pegasus, and Cetus

How to Draw Cetus

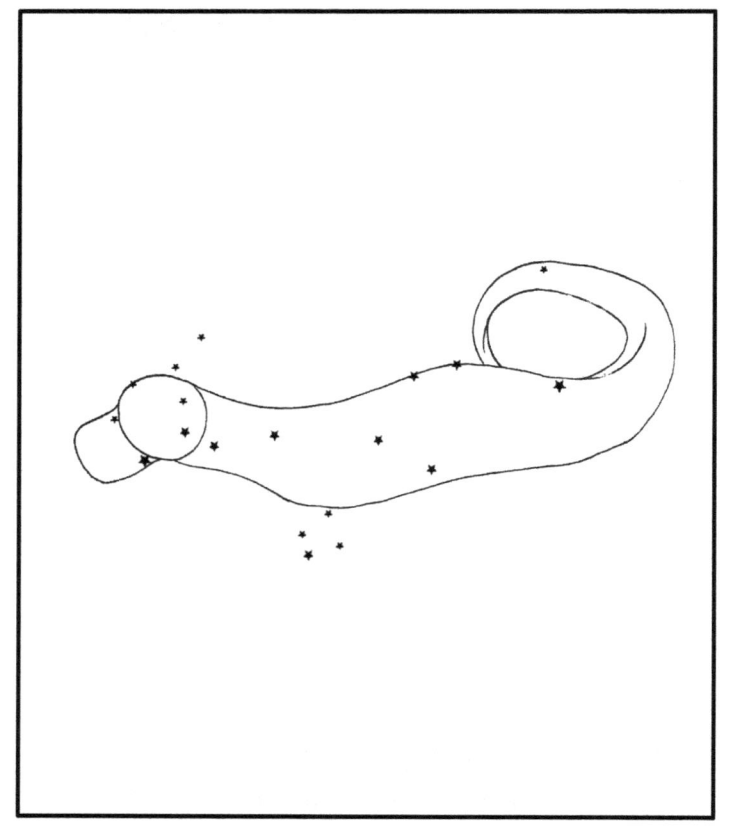

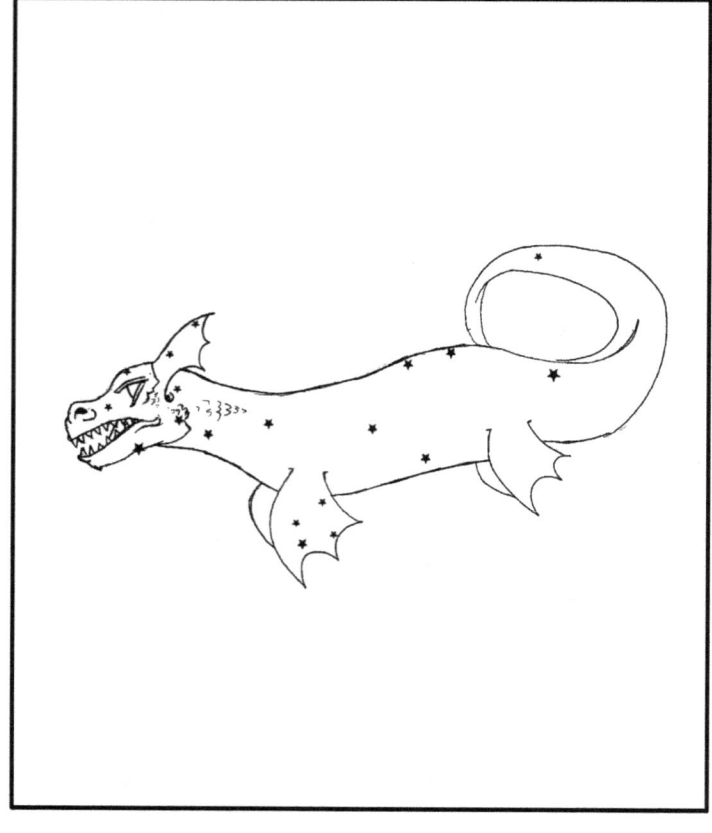

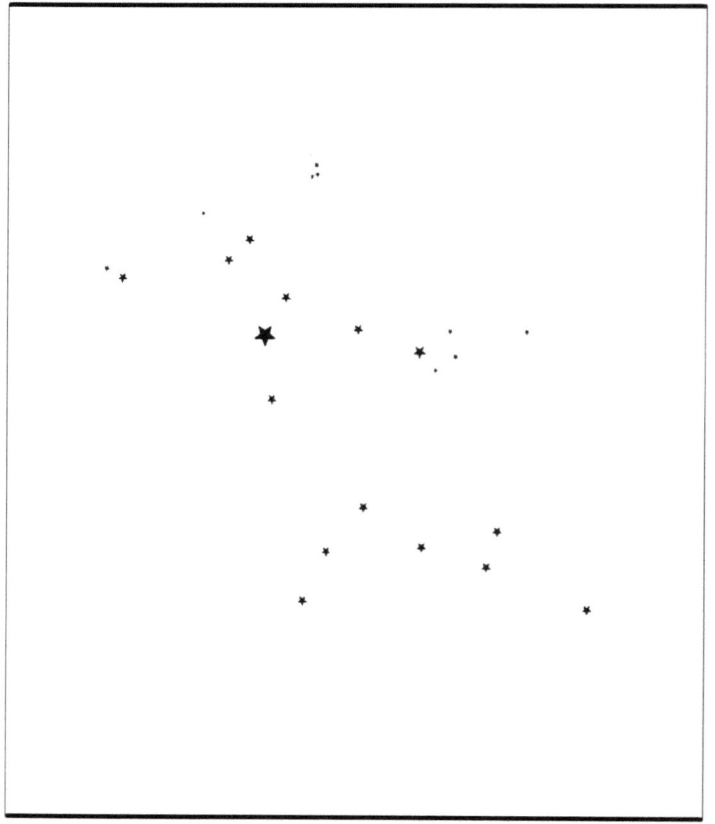

How to Draw Pegasus

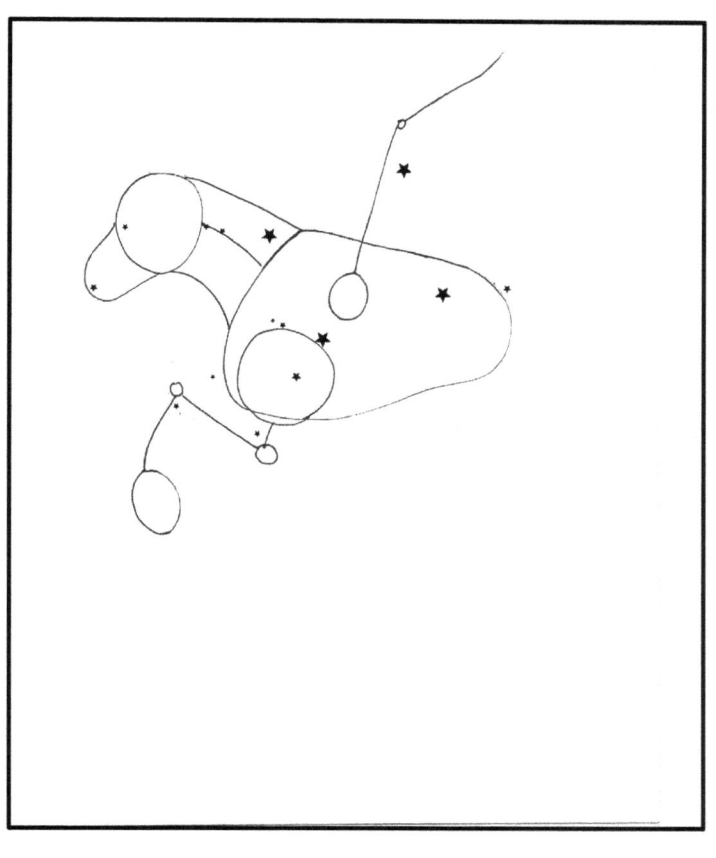

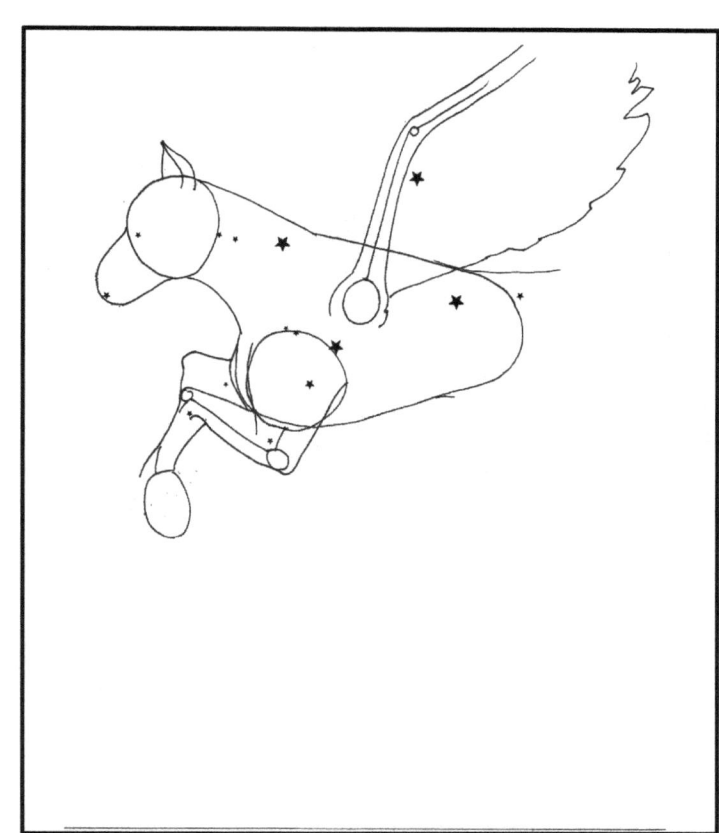

How to Draw Perseus

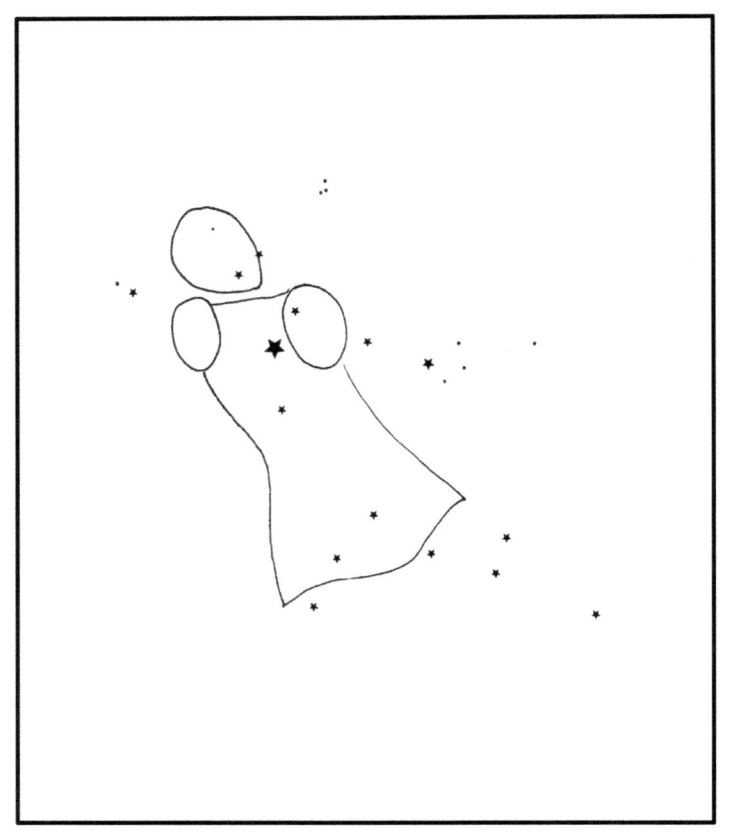

How to Draw Perseus

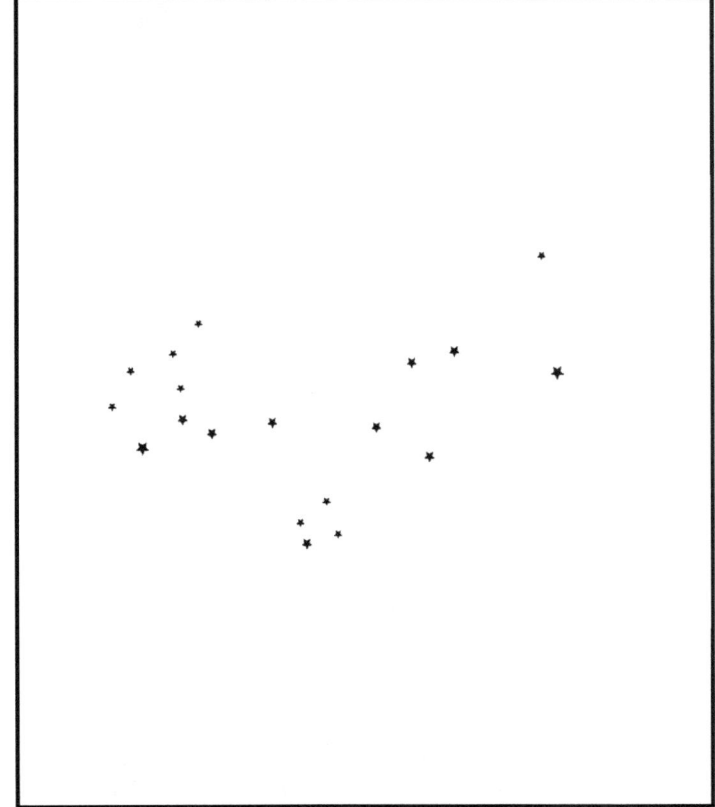

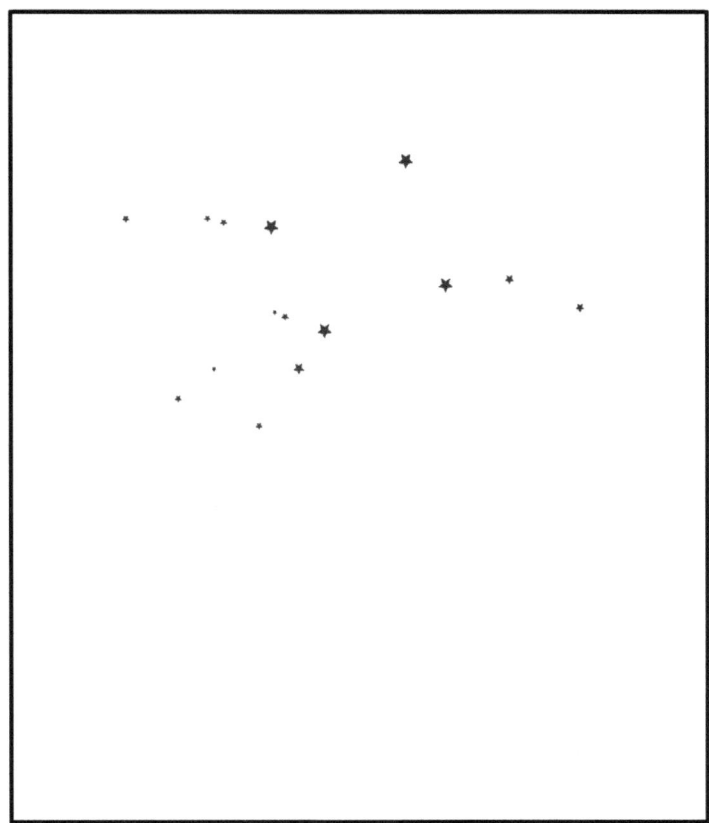

Homework Drawing

I was able to see: ☐ Cetus ☐ Perseus ☐ Pegasus
Make sure to identify the constellations!

Zodiac pt.3

Zodiac pt.3

How to Draw Taurus

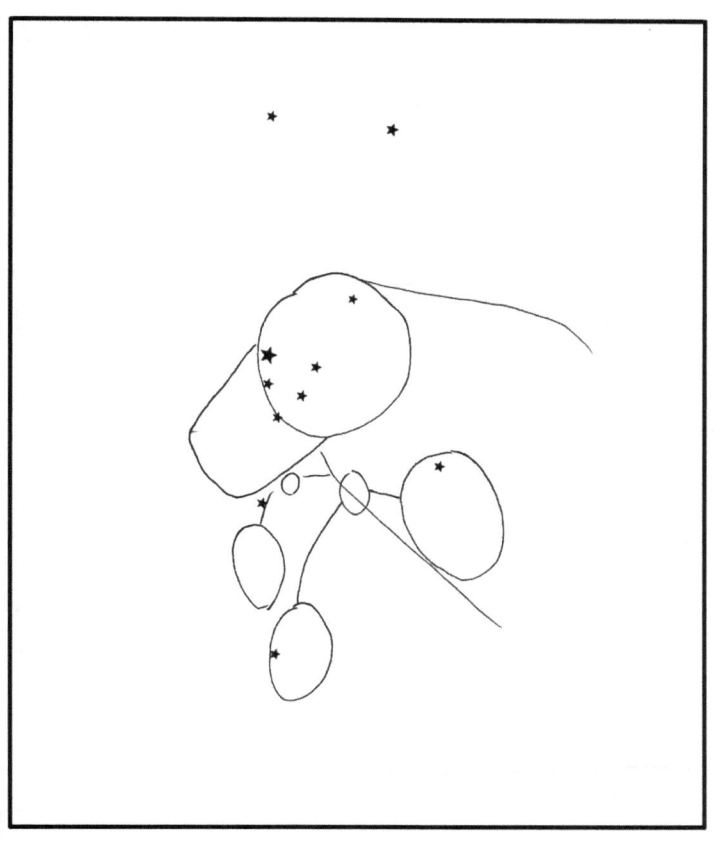

How to Draw Gemini

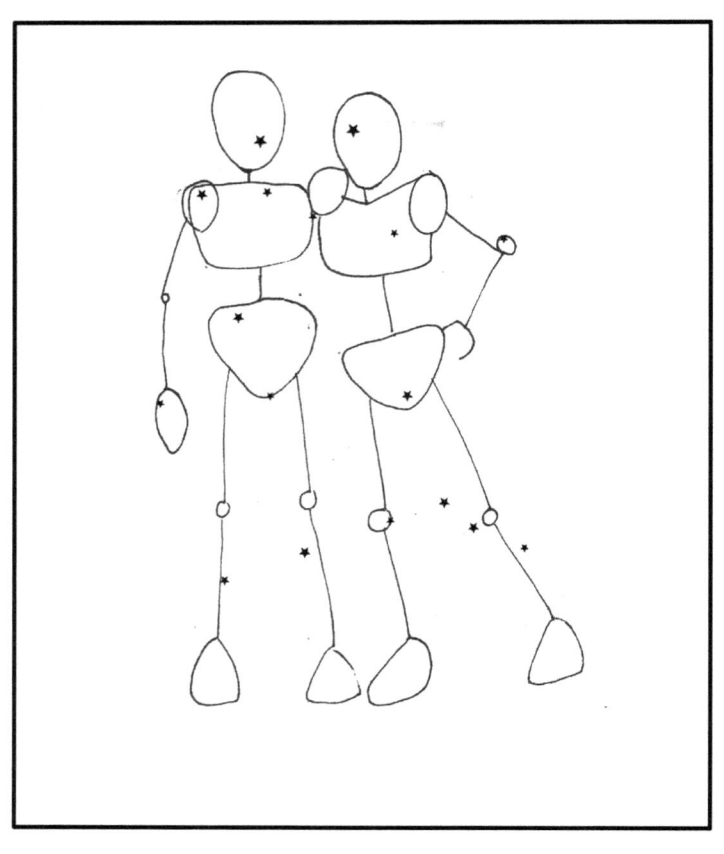

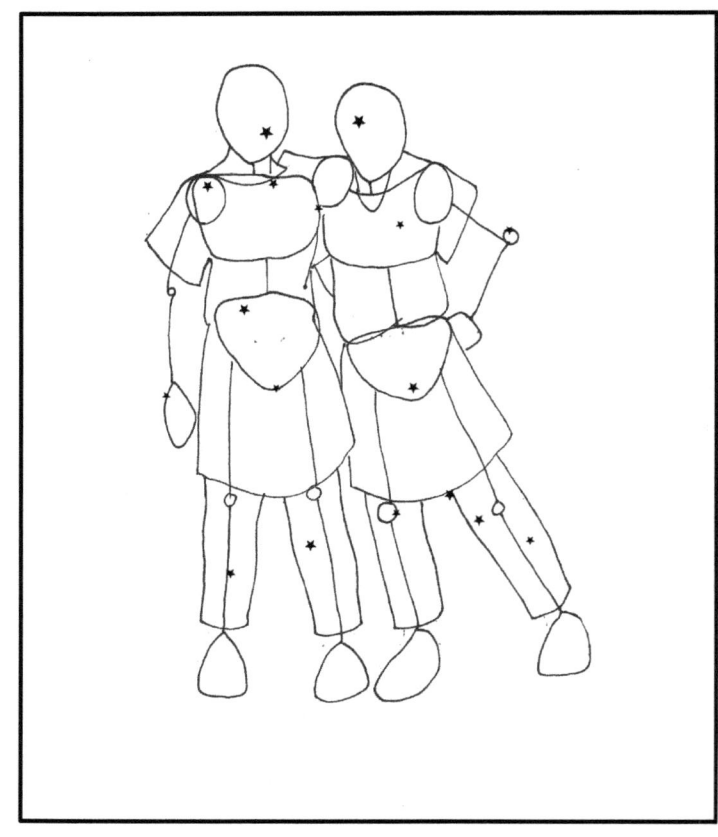

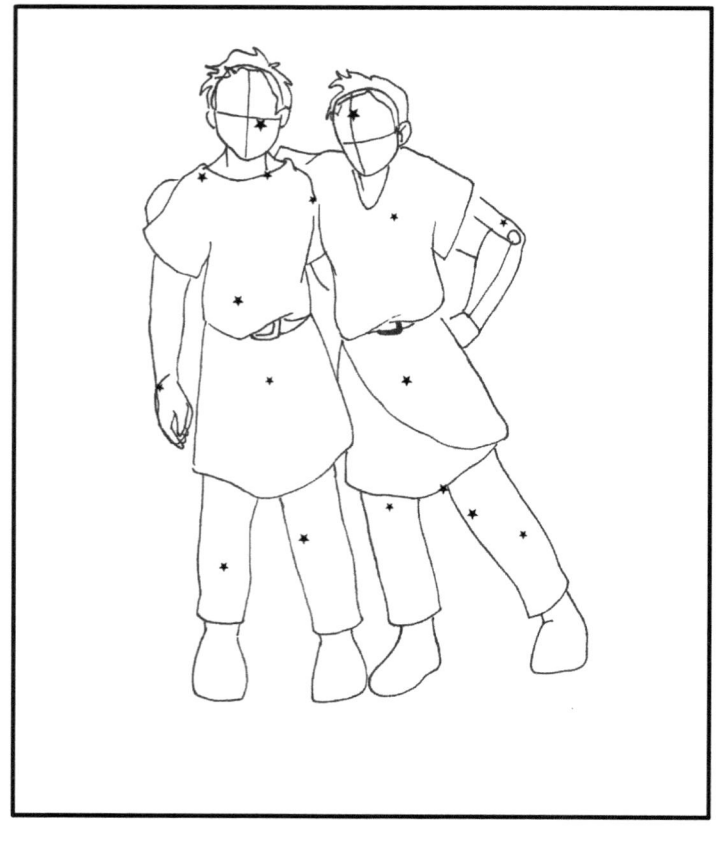

How to Draw Cancer

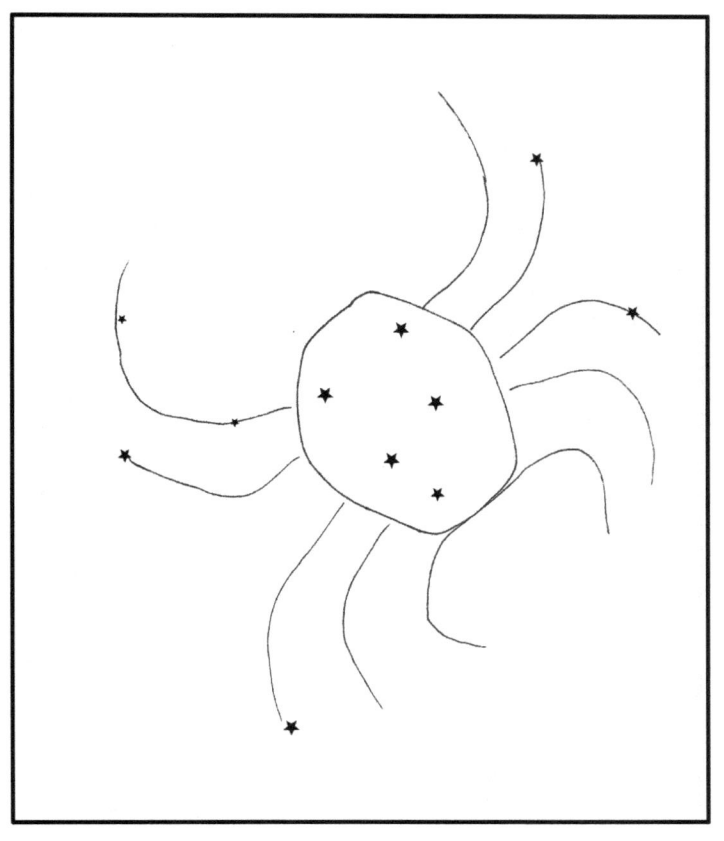

Practice

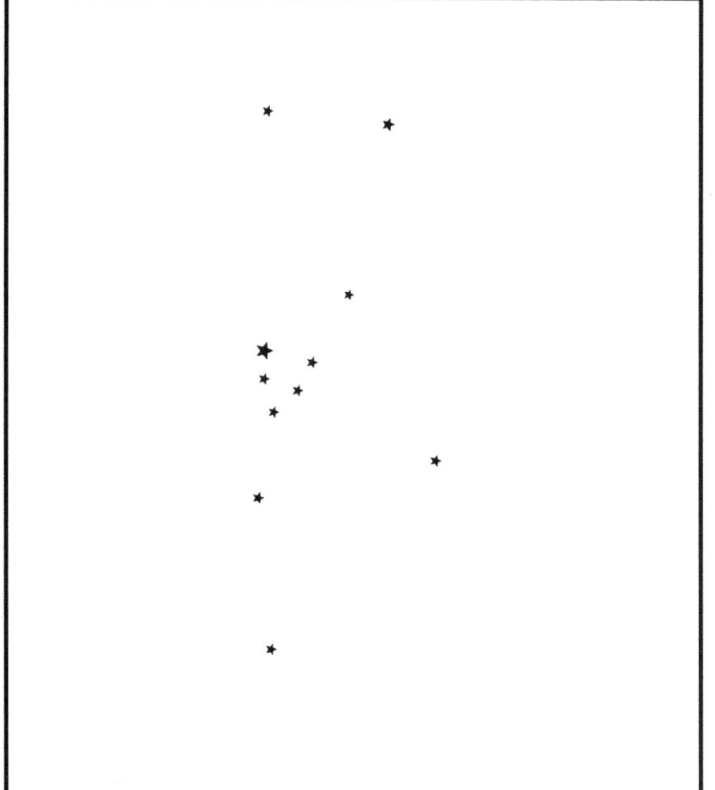
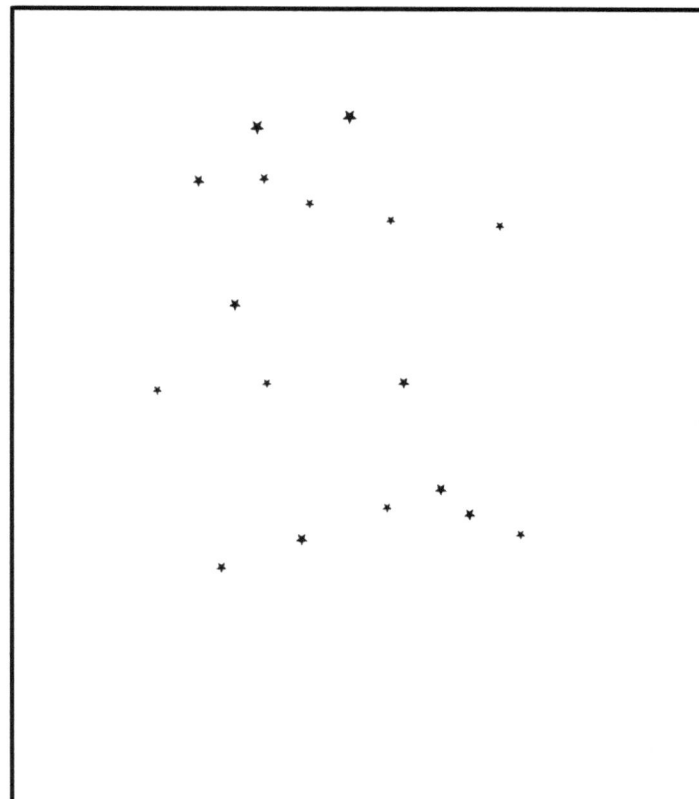
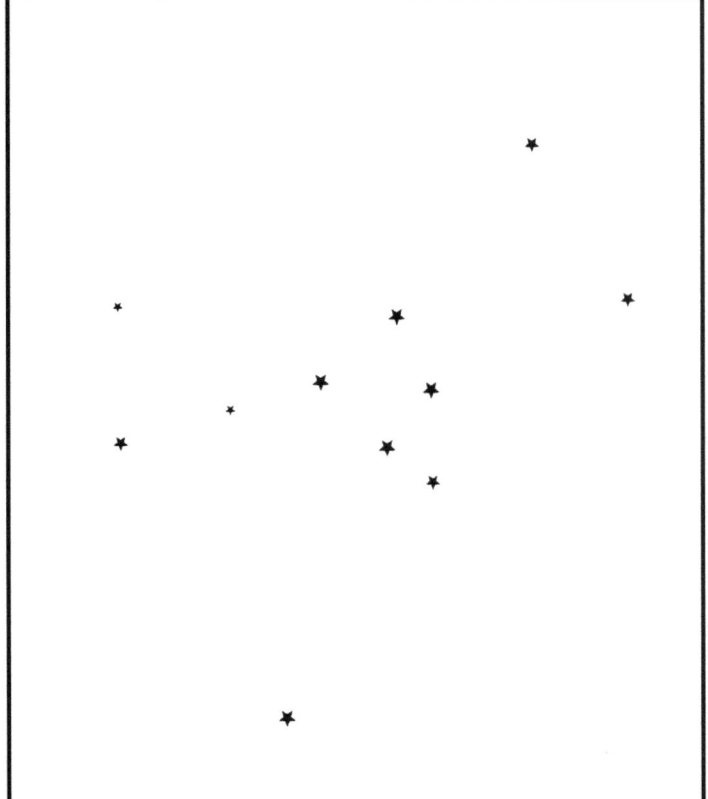
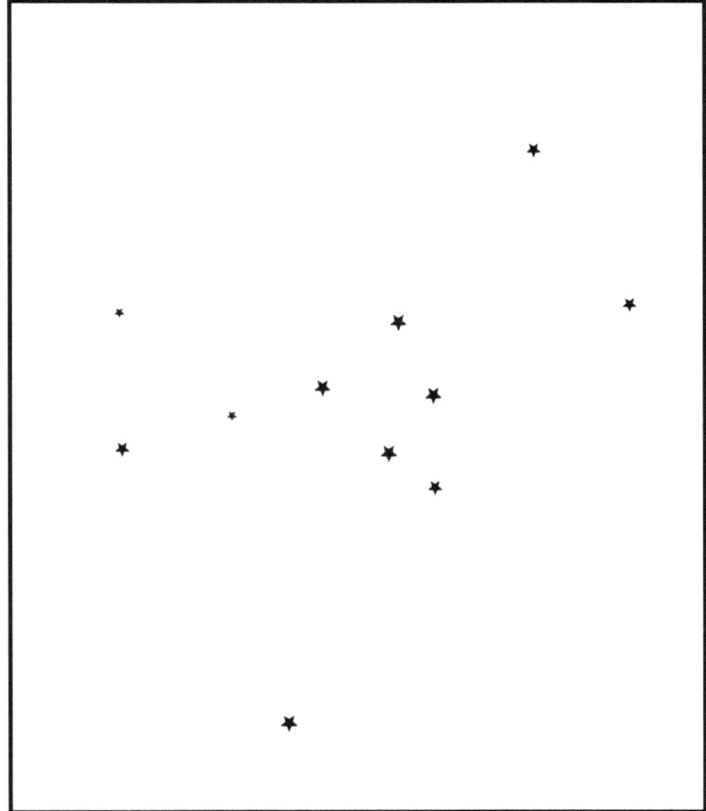

Homework Drawing

I was able to see: ☐ Taurus ☐ Gemini   ☐ Cancer
Make sure to identify the constellations!

Zodiac pt.3

Zodiac pt.3

How to Draw Taurus

How to Draw Gemini

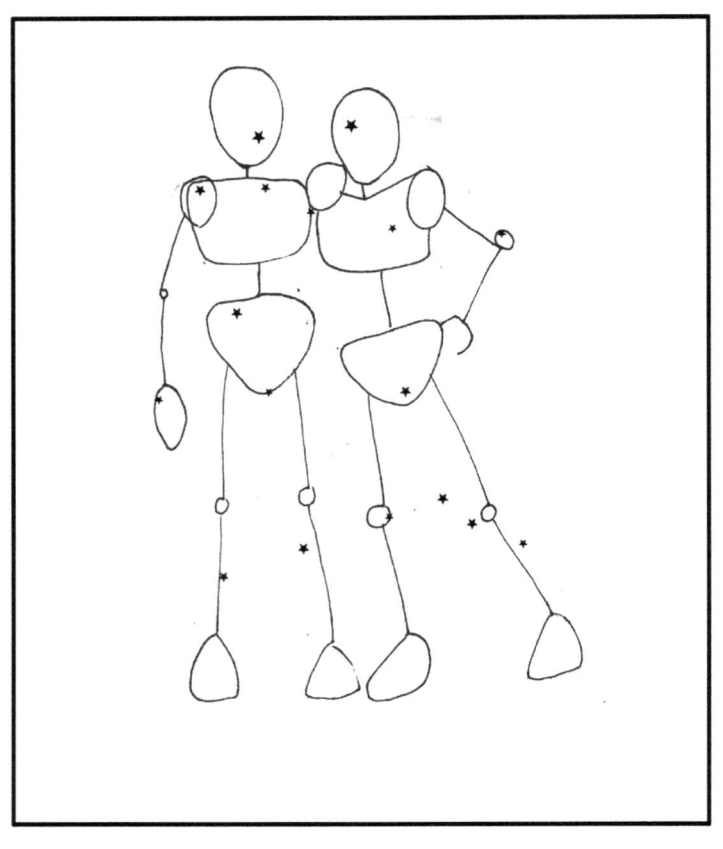

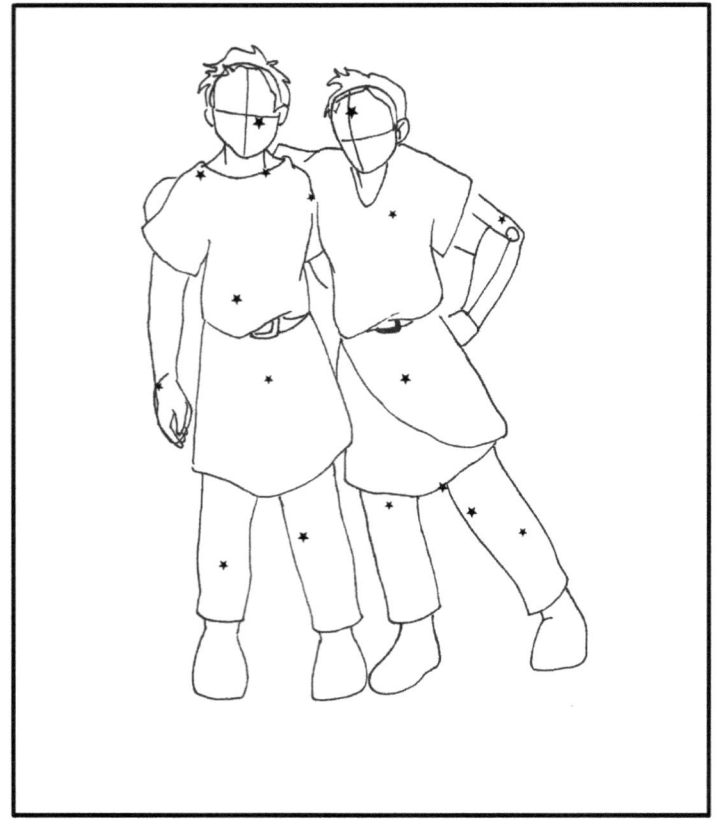

How to Draw Cancer

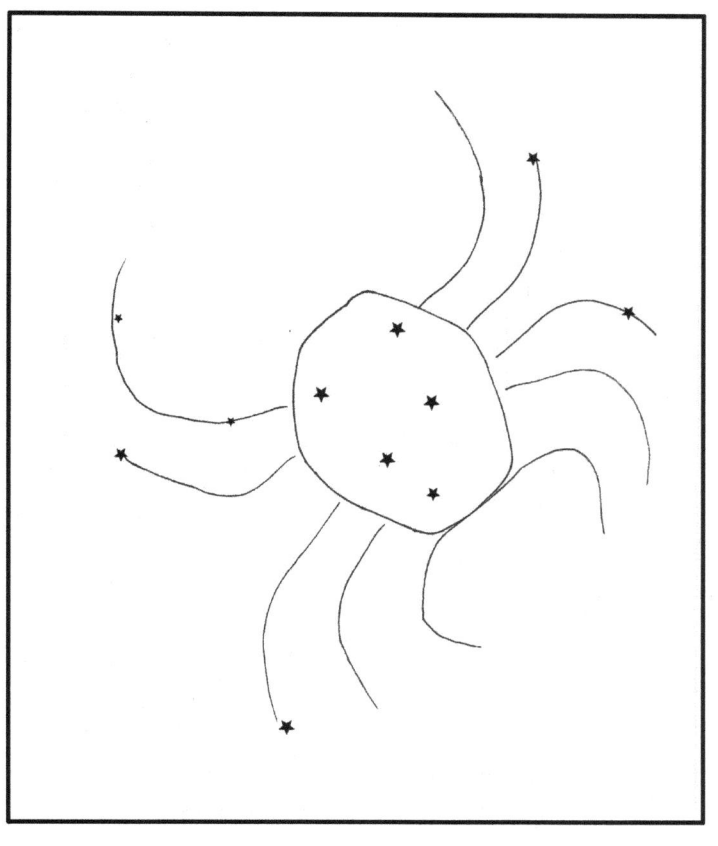

Practice

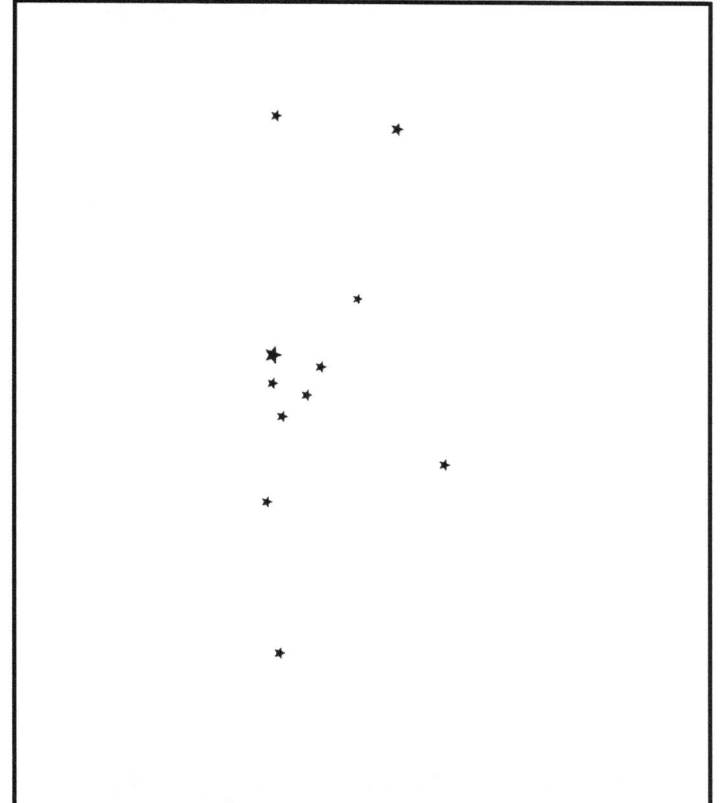

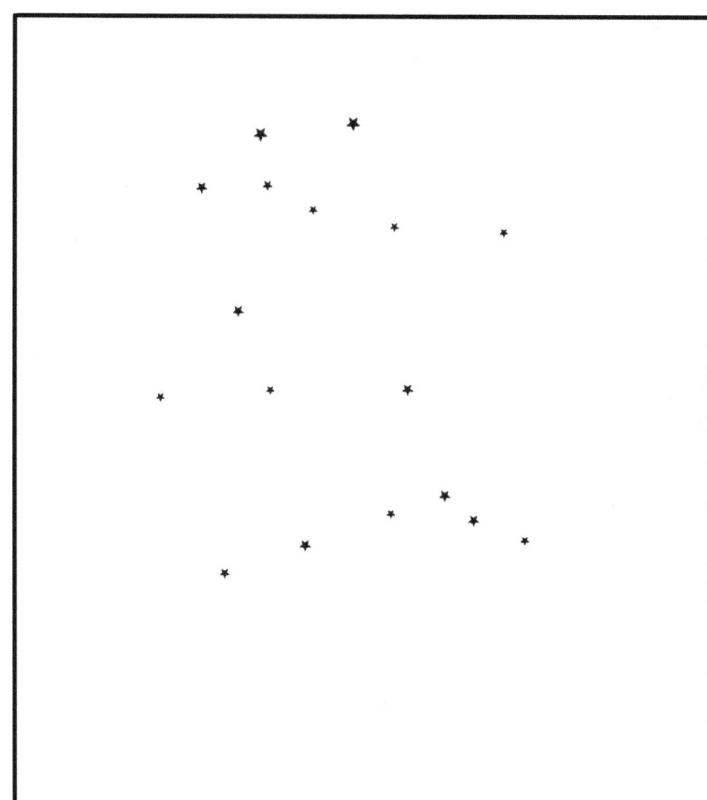

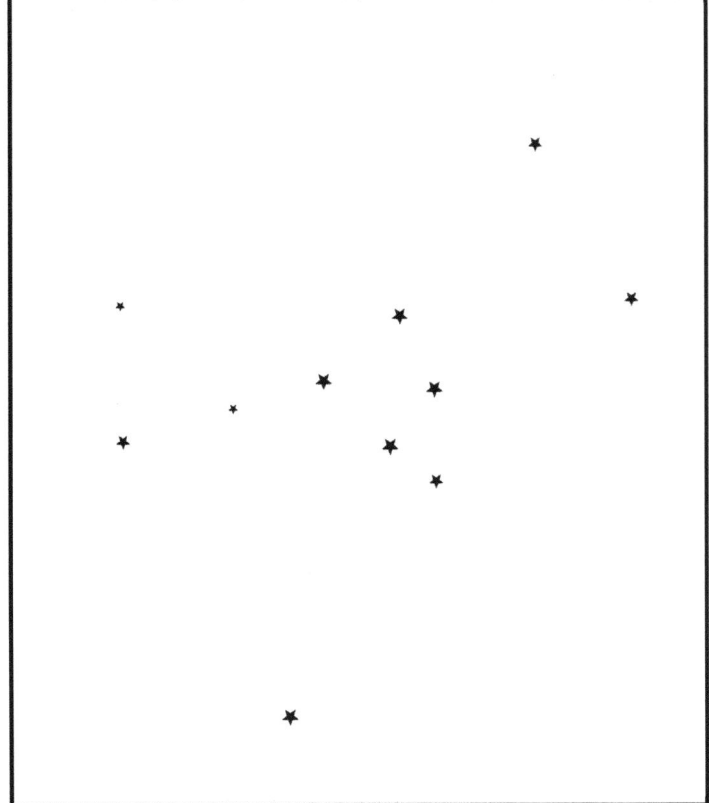

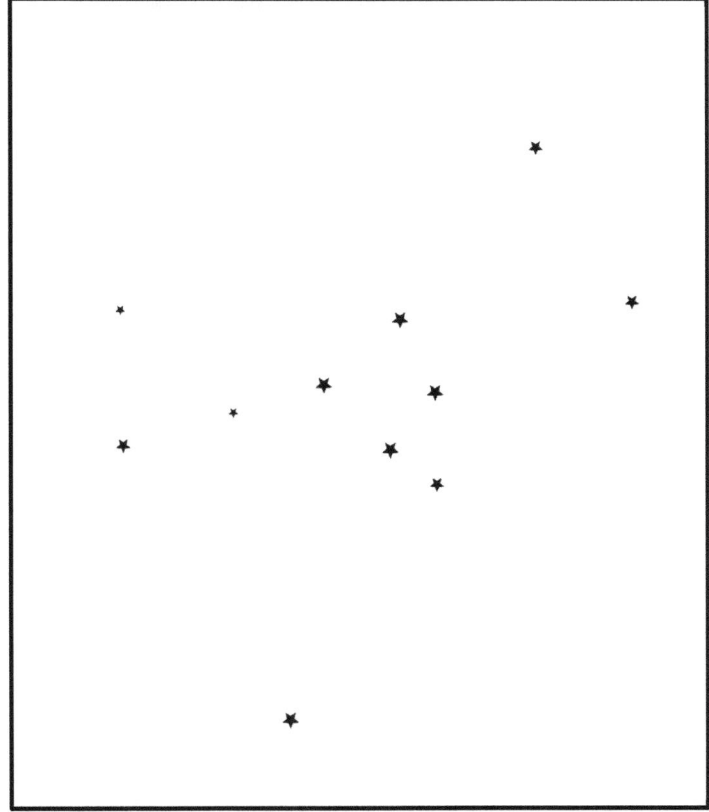

Canis Major, Canis Minor, Auriga

Canis Major, Canis Minor, Auriga

How to Draw Canis minor

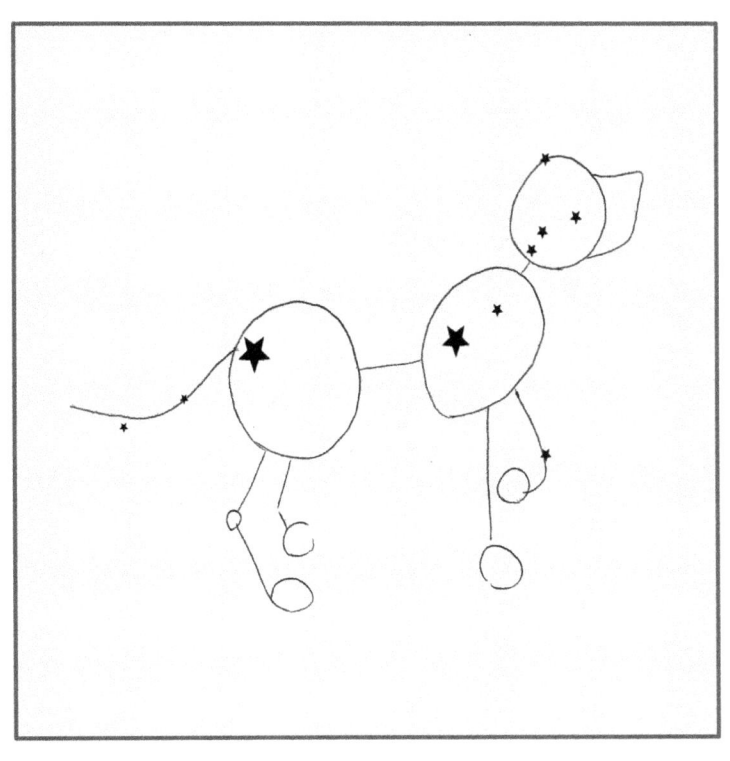

How to Draw Canis Major

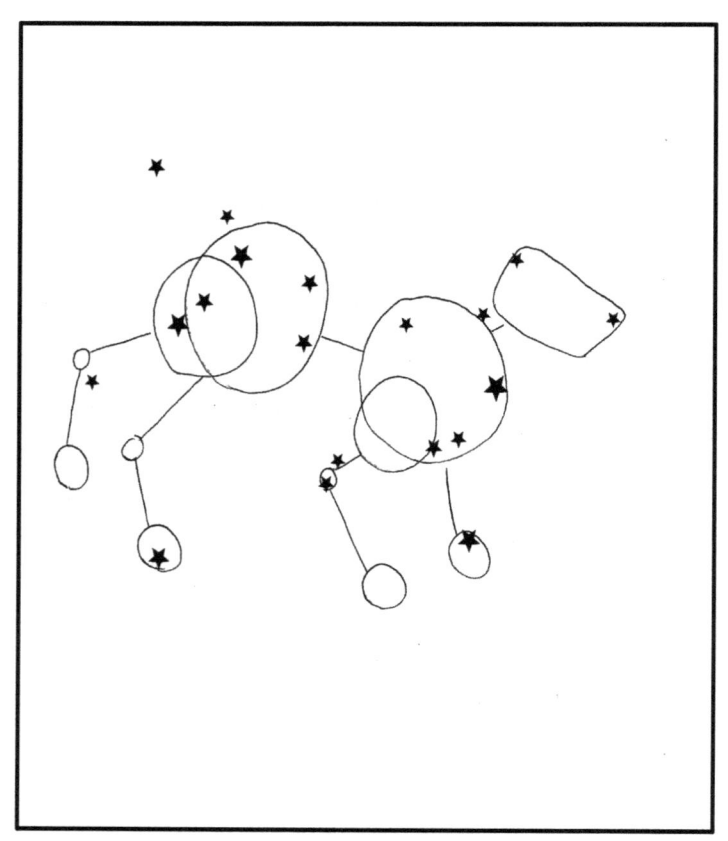

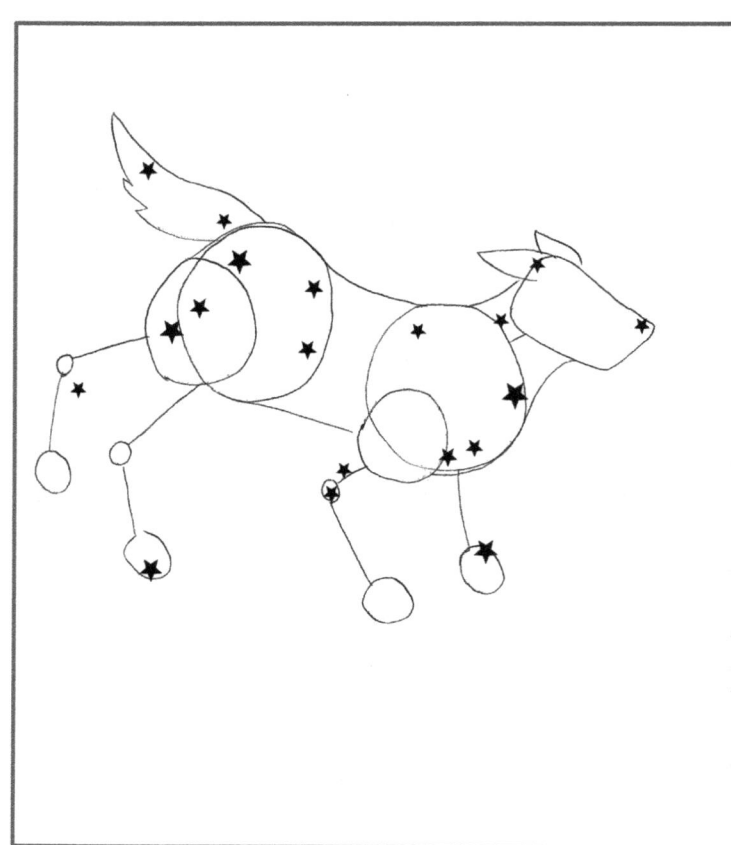

How to Draw Auriga

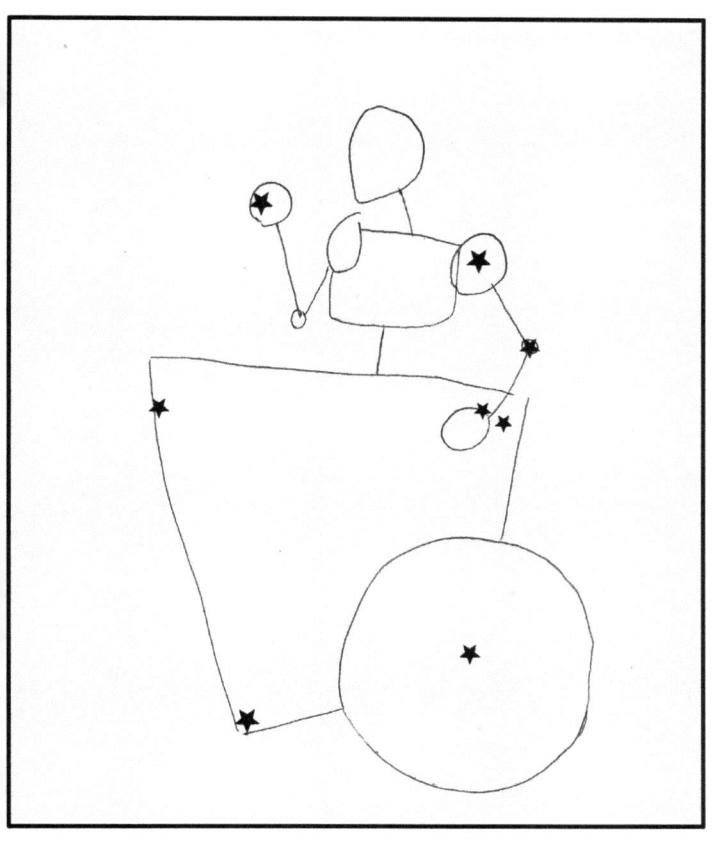

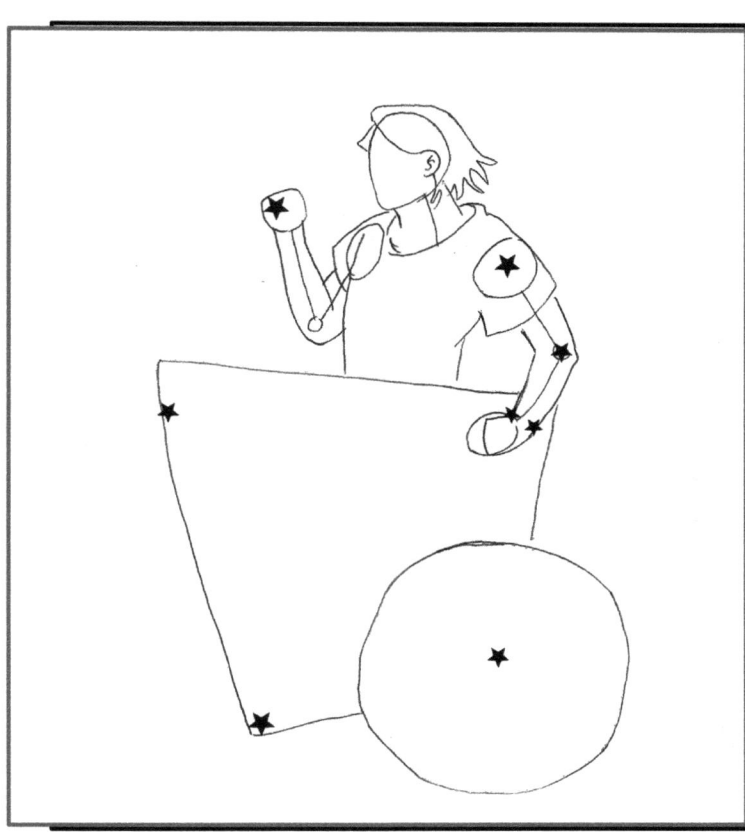

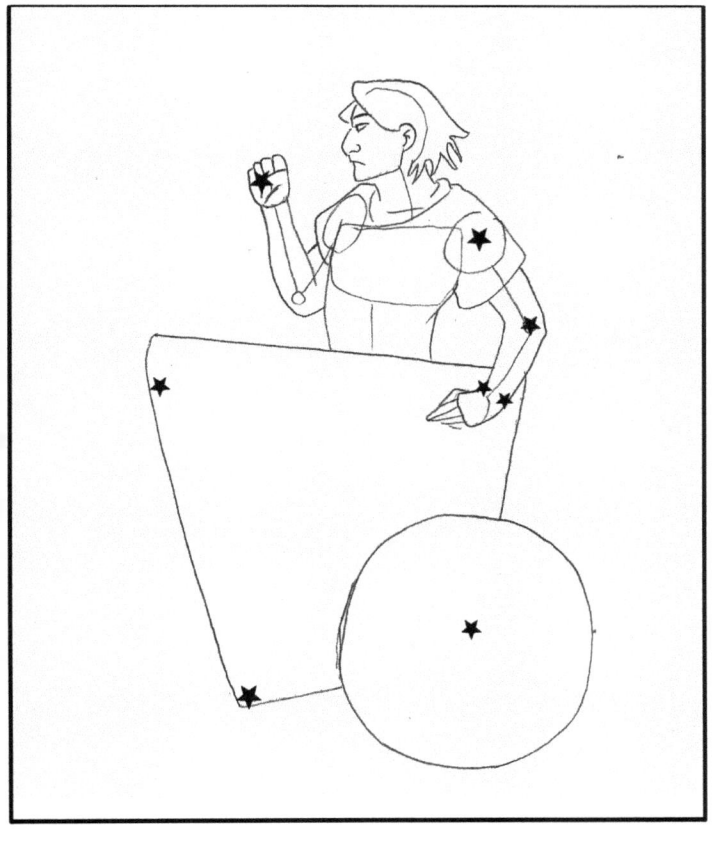

Practice

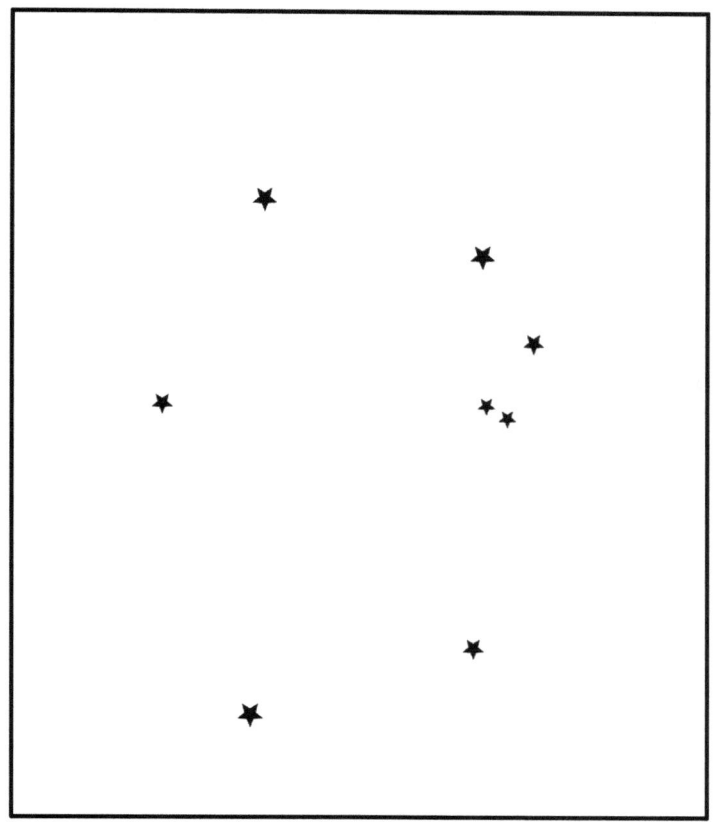

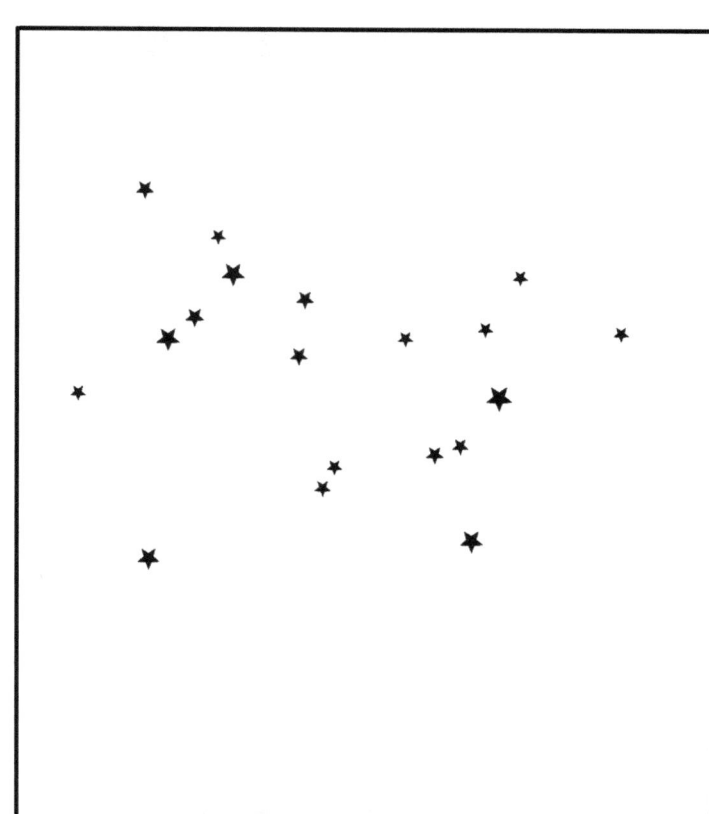

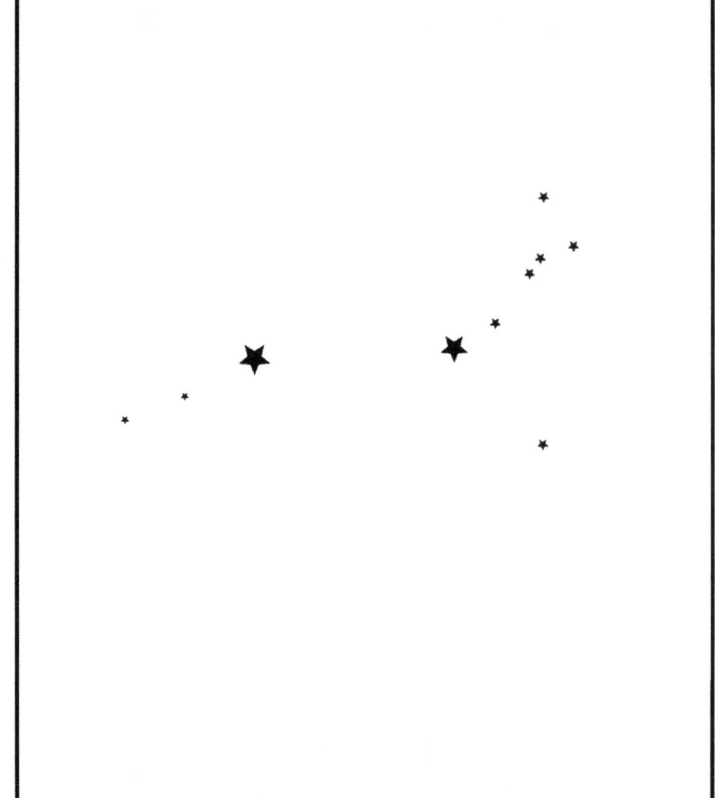

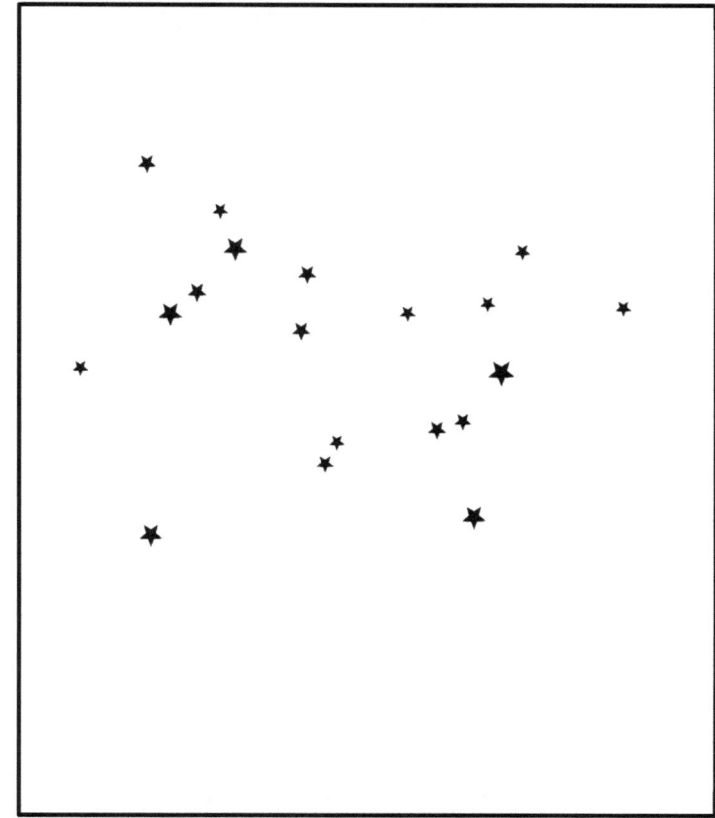

Homework Drawing

I was able to see: ☐ Canis Major, ☐ Canis Minor, ☐ Auriga
Make sure to identify the constellations!

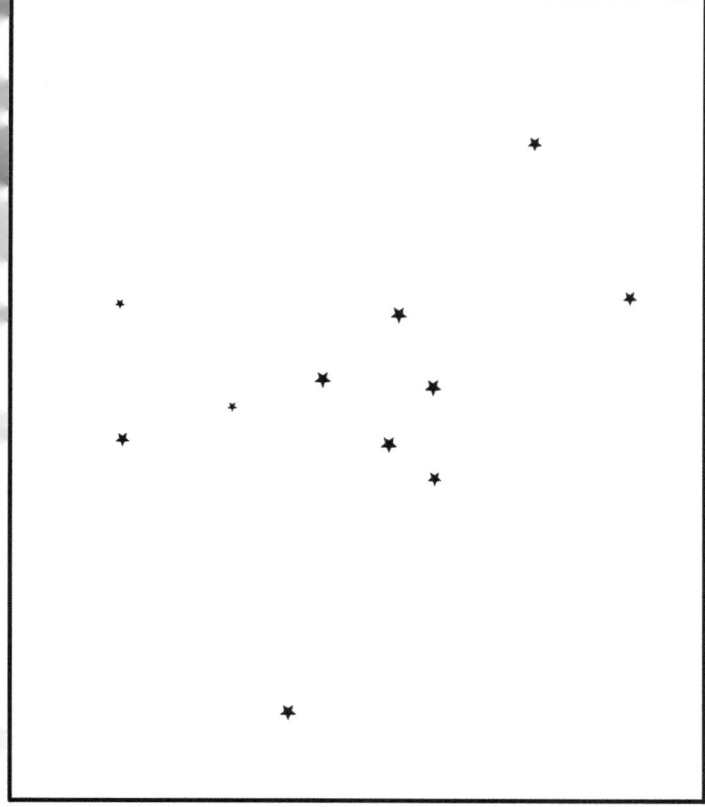

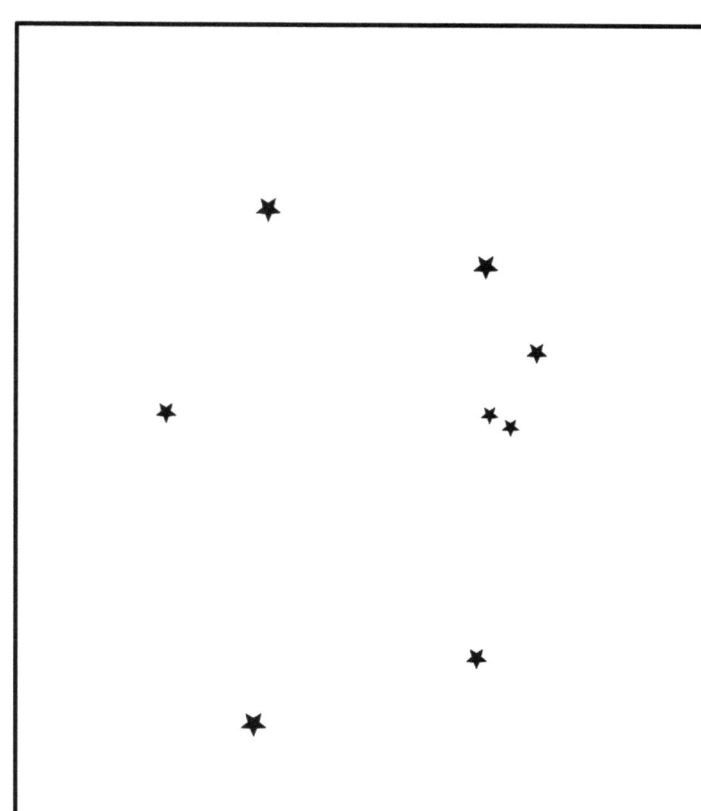

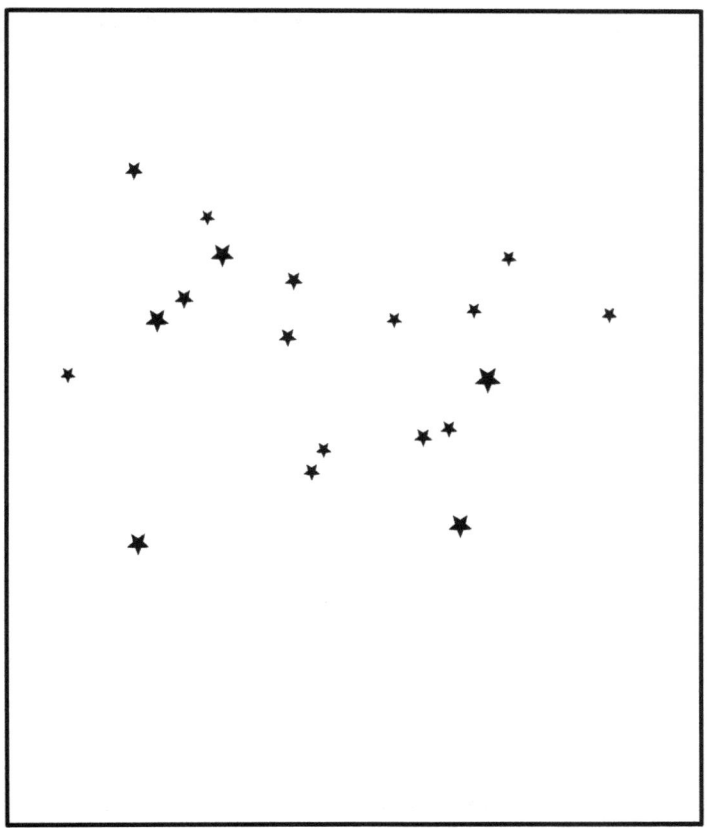

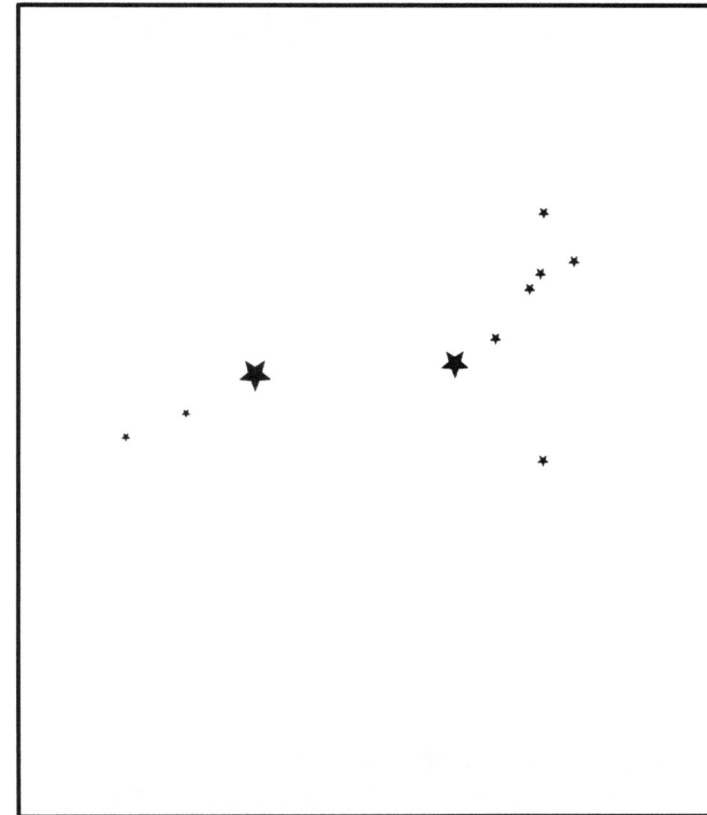

Jupiter

Jupiter is the _____ planet in line from the Sun.

Jupiter has _____ moons.

What is the average temperature on Jupiter? _____

How long is one day on Jupiter? _____

How long is one year on Jupiter? _____

Other interesting things about Jupiter:
Jupiter is huge! _____ Earths could fit inside Jupiter! Jupiter is the first of the "Gas Giants" huge planets past the Asteroid belt. These planets have a tiny solid core, surrounded by gas. For Jupiter this gas is mostly helium, methane, and water. Jupiter had several rings, but they are so faint one can barely see them!

One notable thing on Jupiter is the Great Storm. This red spot is larger than Earth and has been a huge storm that has lasted over 300 years!

Saturn

Saturn is the _____ planet in line from the Sun.

Saturn has _____ moons.

What is the average temperature on Saturn? _____

How long is one day on Saturn? _____

How long is one year on Saturn? _____

Other interesting things about Saturn:
Saturn is the second of the gas giants. It's gaseous body is mostly made from Hydrogen and Helium. This means Saturn is extremely light! If you had a bathtub large enough to fit Saturn, Saturn would float! Saturn also has nine large rings. These rings are mostly made of ice and dust, but are believed to have been created when two of Saturn's moons crashed into each other and broke apart.

Uranus

Uranus is the _____ planet in line from the Sun.

Uranus has _____ moons.

What is the average temperature on Uranus? _____

How long is one day on Uranus? _____

How long is one year on Uranus? _____

Other interesting things about Uranus:
Uranus is the first planet to have been discovered! All the other planets were known since ancient times, but Uranus was discovered in 1781 by William Herschel. She can technically be seen without a telescope, but you would need very good eyes! She is known as the sideways planet because she is tilted 90 degrees! This means that her north and south poles face the sun! Uranus is a special type of Gas Giant, known as an Ice Giant because underneath her gaseous exterior she has a huge ocean of ice. Uranus also has faint rings. The inner rings are narrow and dark. The outer rings are brightly colored and easier to see.
Uranus has many moons, the five major moons are Miranda, Ariel, Umbriel, Titania, and Oberon. Notice anything about the names?

Neptune

Neptune is the _____ planet in line from the Sun.

Neptune has _____ moons.

What is the average temperature on Neptune? _____

How long is one day on Neptune? _____

How long is one year on Neptune? _____

Other interesting things about Saturn:
Neptune is our solar system's windiest world. Winds whip clouds of frozen methane across the planet at speeds of more than 2,000 km/h (1,200 mph)—close to the top speed of a U.S. Navy F/A-18 Hornet fighter jet. Neptune is very similar to Uranus. He has a thick layer of ice surrounding a rocky core. Neptune is the only planet in our solar system not visible the naked eye and the only one discovered by Math! Urbain-Jean-Joseph Le Verrier noticed some irregularities in Uranus' orbit, He then figured out that there must be another planet pulling on Uranus and calculated the exact spot the planet would be!

Neptune has one major moon Triton. Spacecraft images show the moon has a sparsely cratered surface with smooth volcanic plains, mounds and round pits formed by icy lava flows.

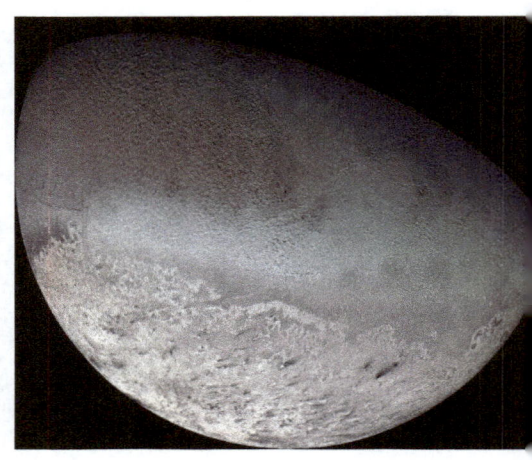

Outer Planets and Space Objects

Planets and distance are not drawn to exact scale.

Planet: _____

Fact 1:
_____
_____
_____

Fact 2:
_____
_____
_____

Planet: _____

Fact 1:
_____
_____
_____

Fact 2:
_____
_____
_____

Planet: _____

Fact 1:
_____
_____
_____

Fact 2:
_____
_____
_____

Planet: _____

Fact 1:
_____
_____
_____

Fact 2:
_____
_____
_____

Moons!

Fact 1:
_____
_____
_____

Fact 2:
_____
_____
_____

Fact 3:
_____
_____
_____

Ursa Major, Ursa Minor, Hydra

Ursa Major, Ursa Minor, Hydra

Ursa Major, Ursa Minor, Hydra

How to Draw Ursa Major

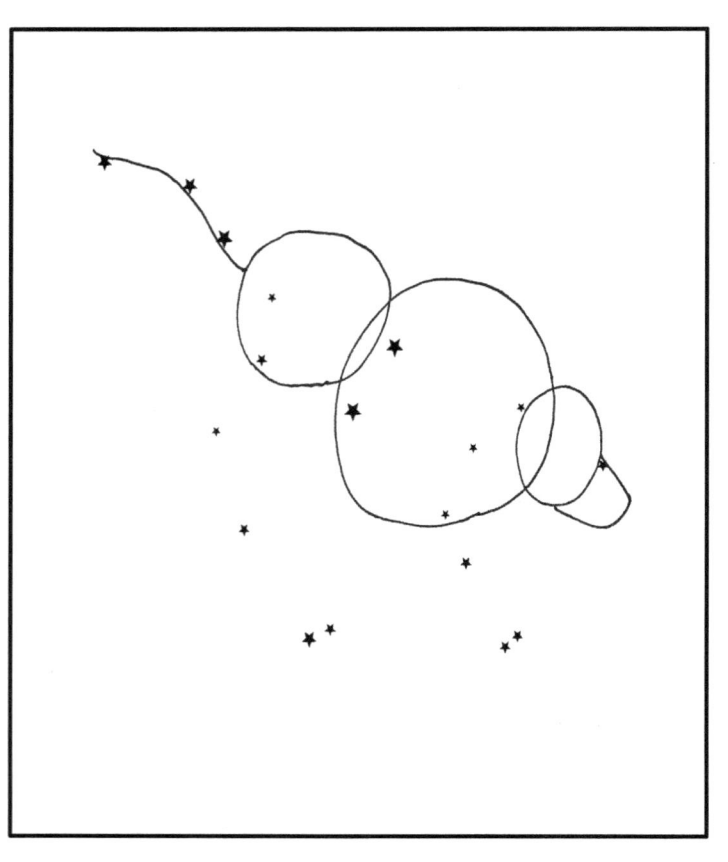

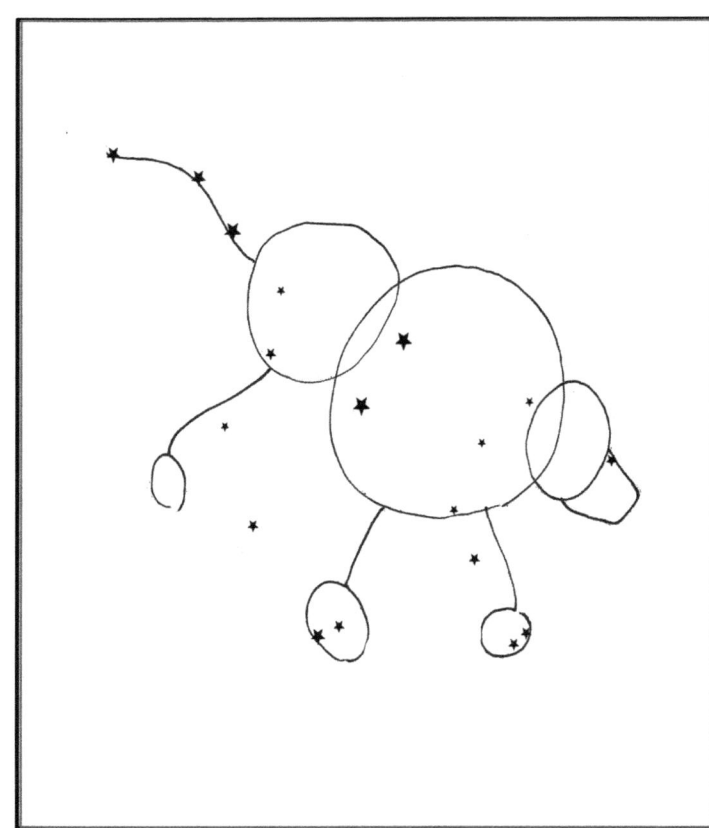

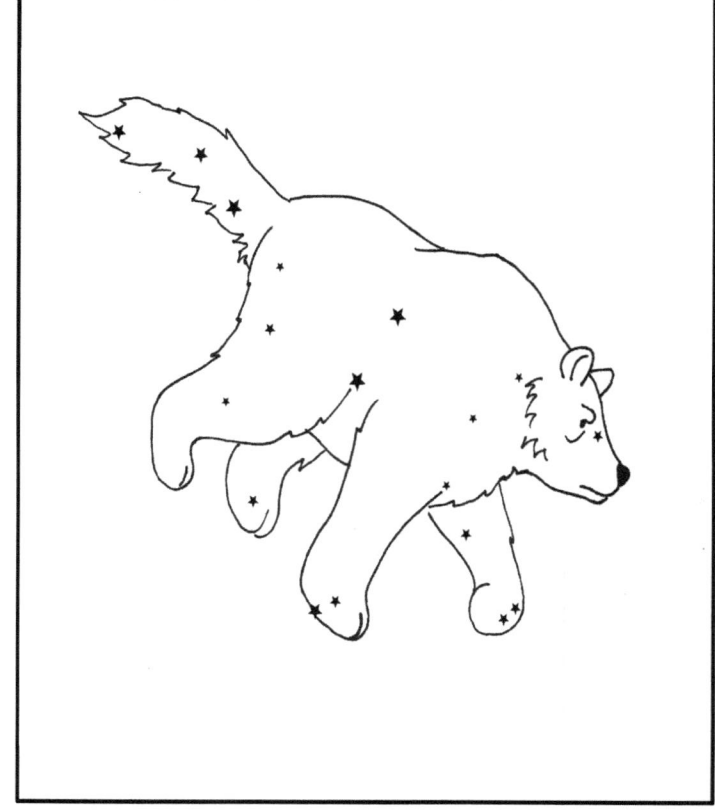

How to Draw Ursa Minor

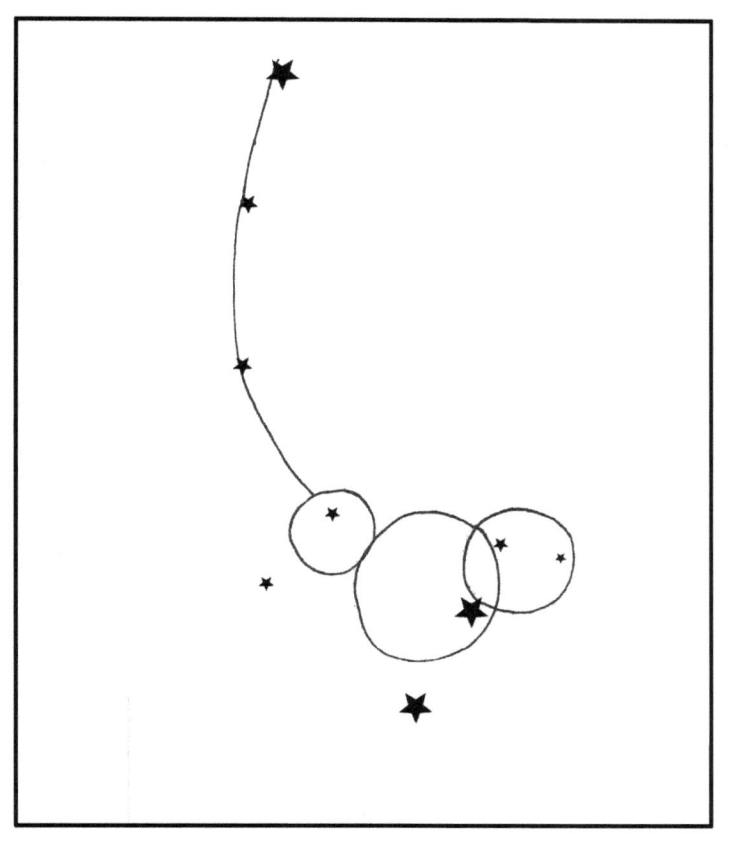

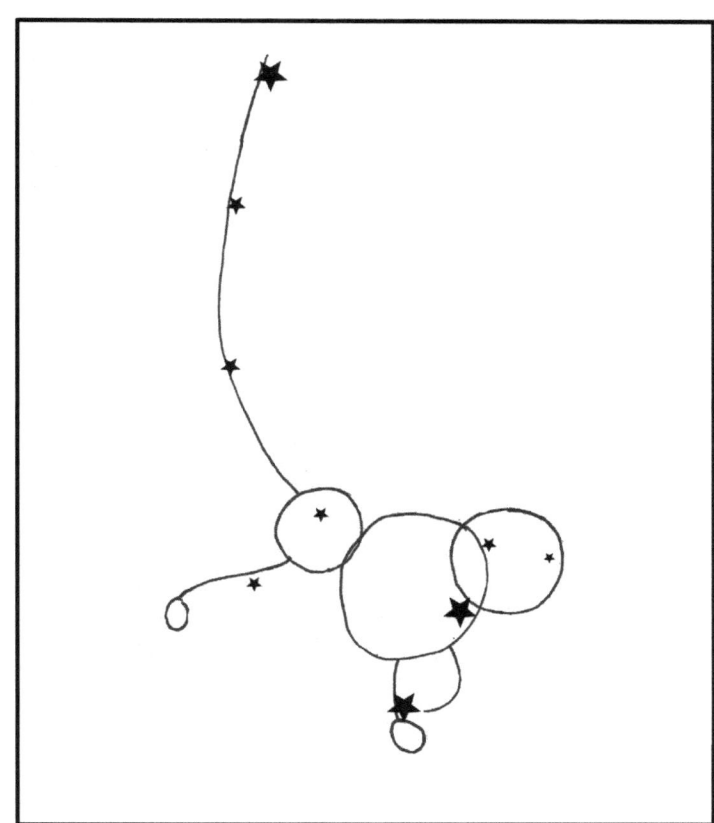

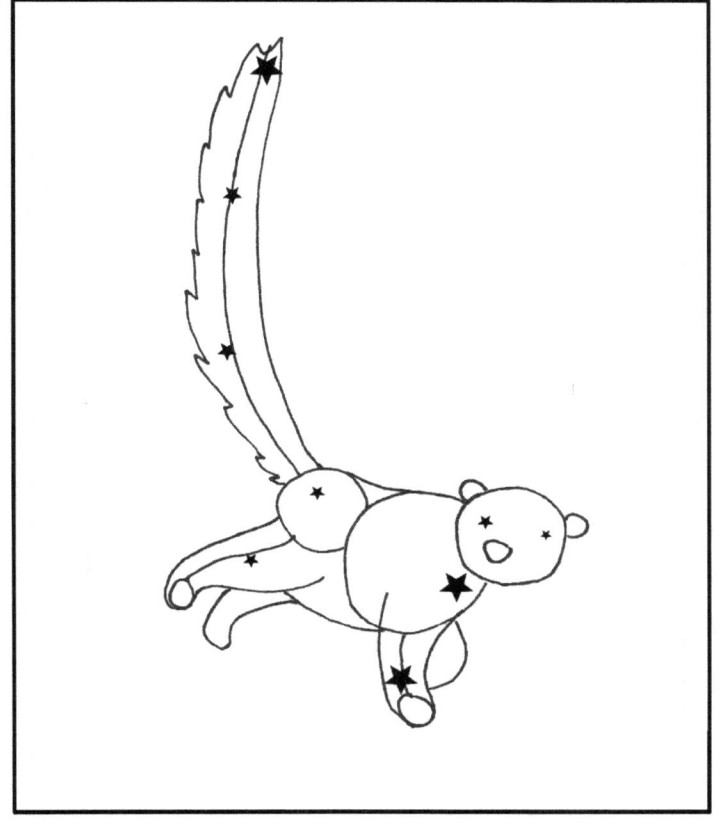

How to Draw Hydra

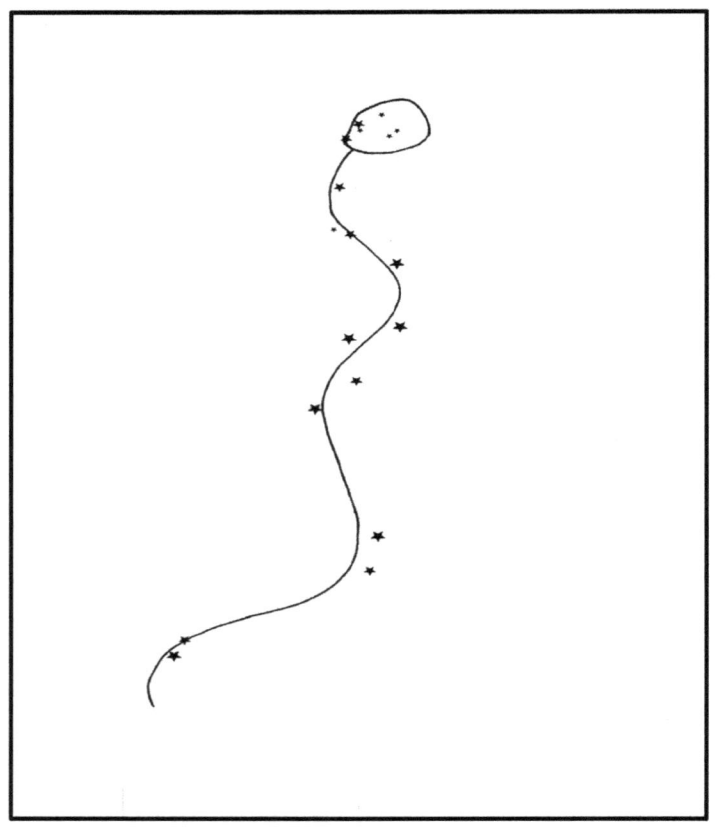

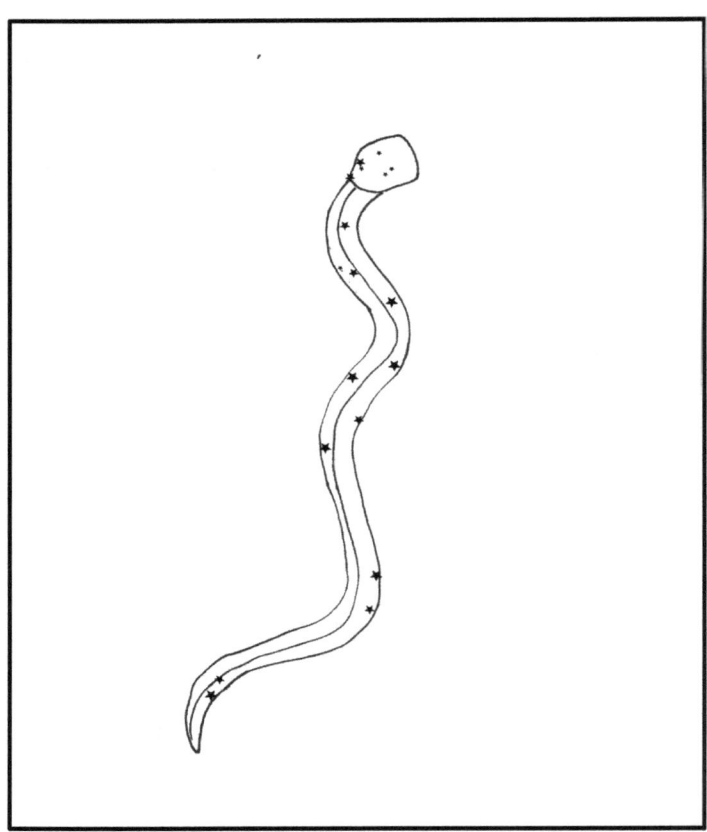

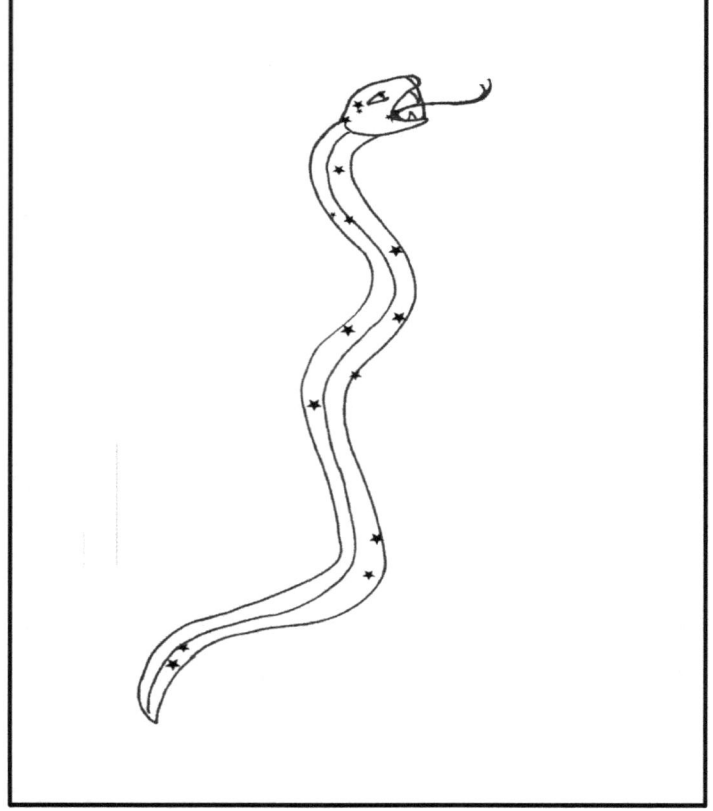

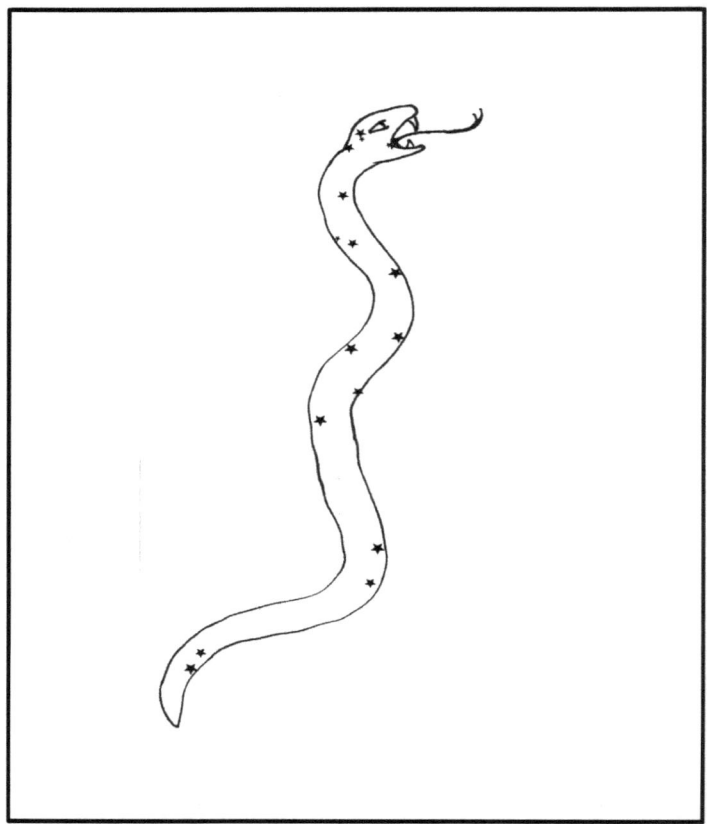

Practice Drawing

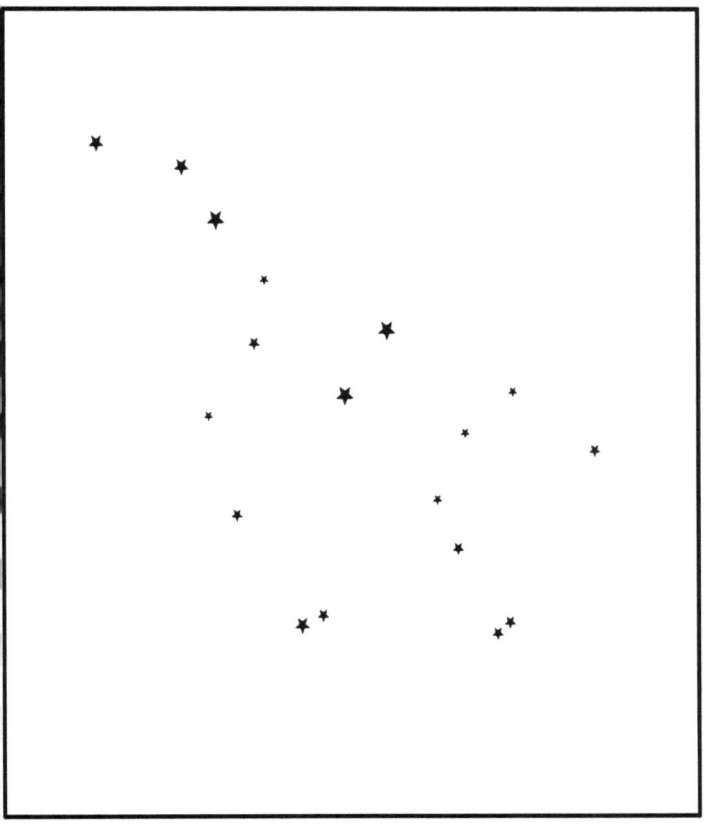

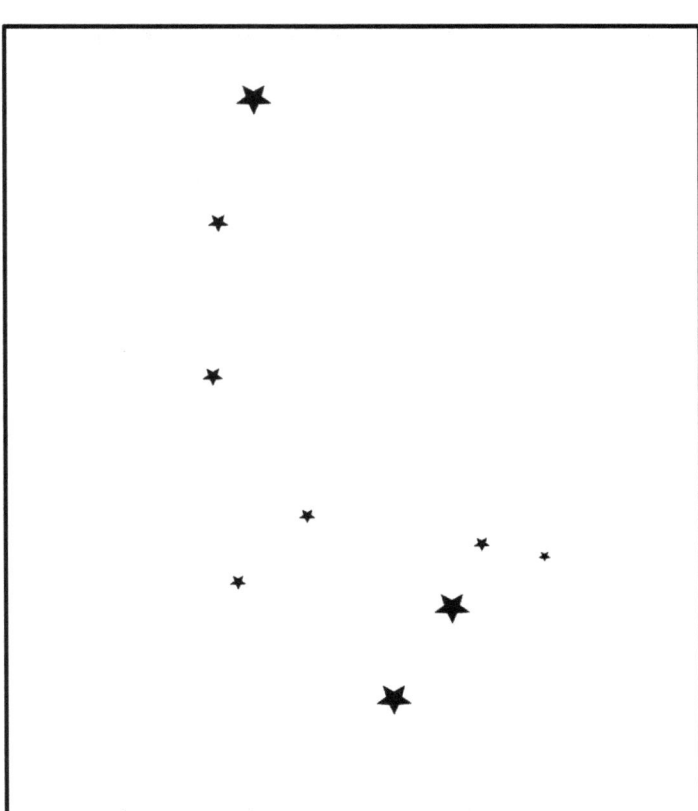

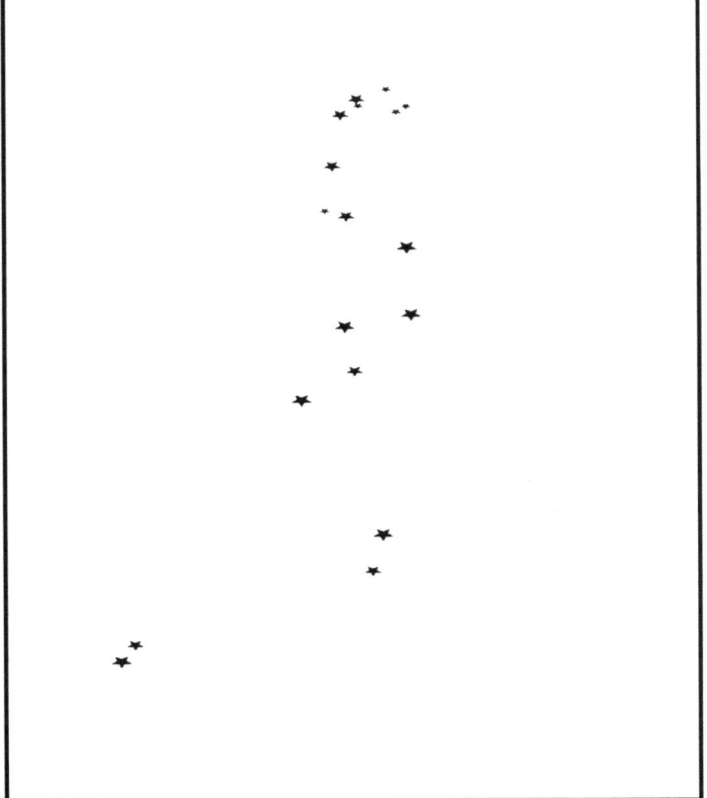

Homework Drawing

I was able to see: ☐ Ursa Major ☐ Ursa Minor ☐ Draco ☐ Hydra

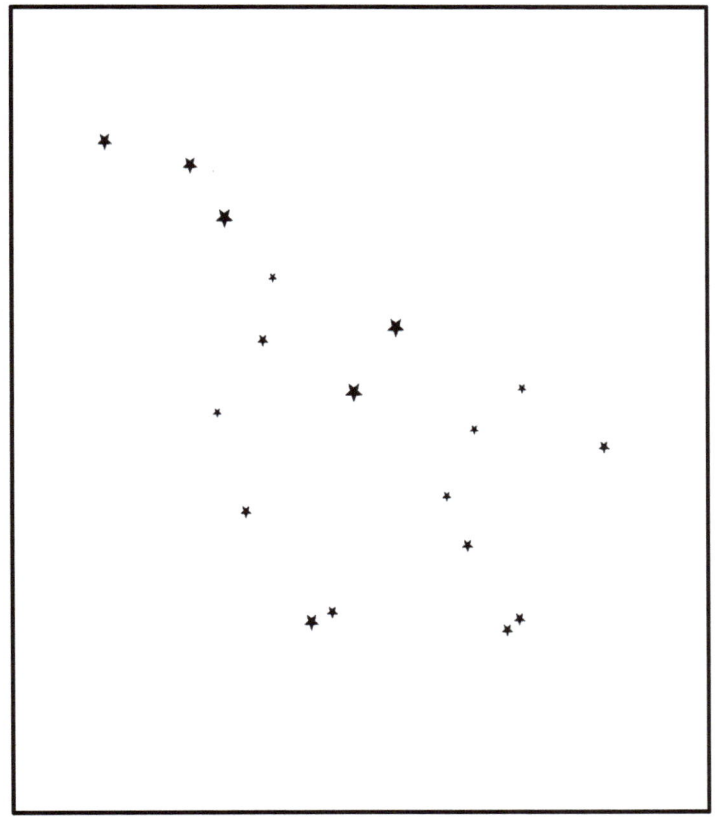

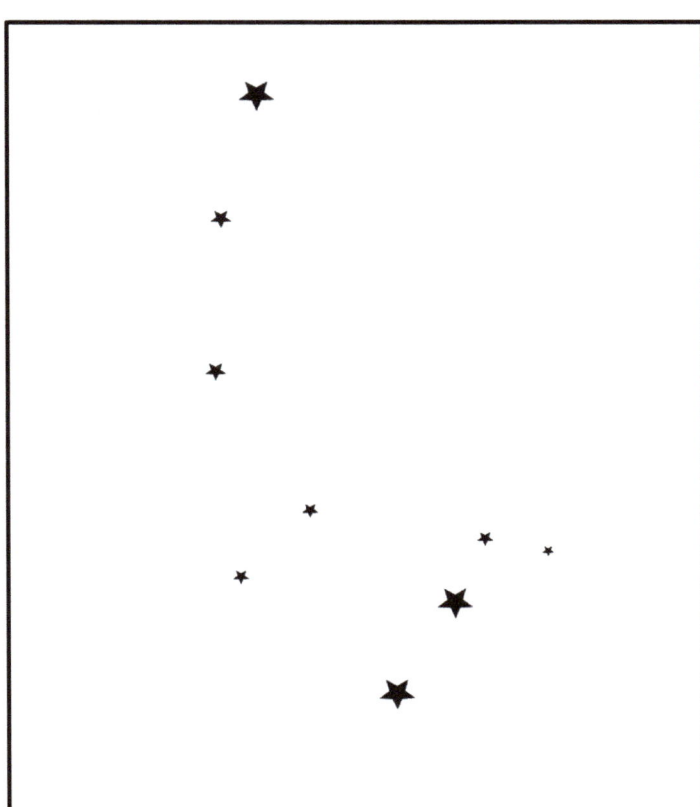

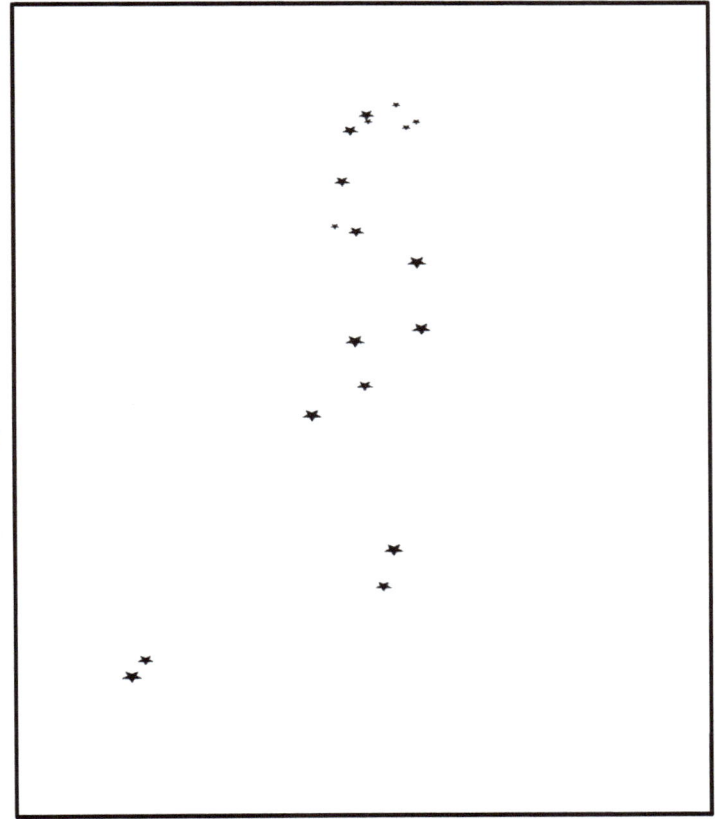

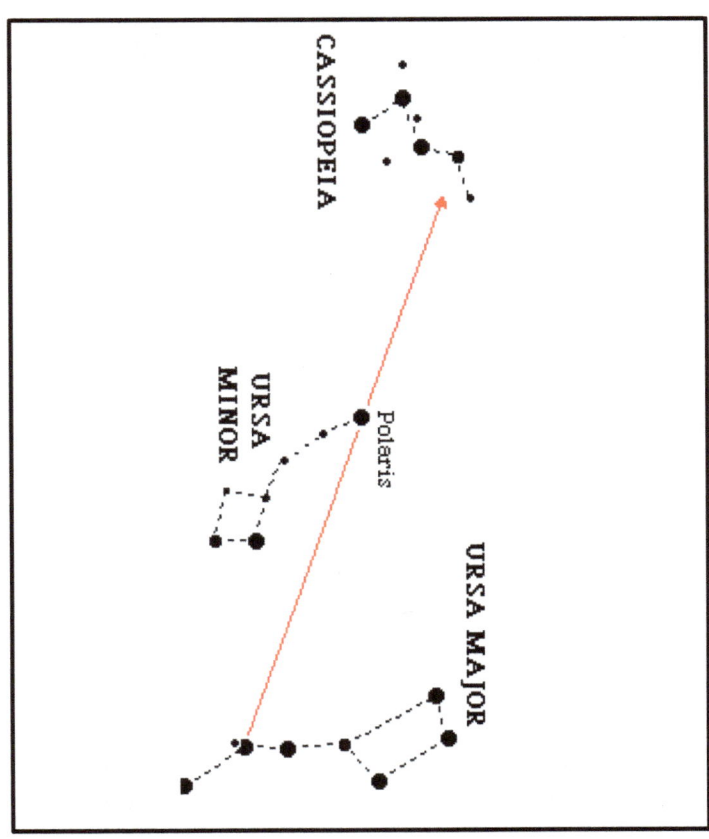

Asteroid Belt Dwarf Planets

Kuiper belt Dwarf Planets

Ceres: Discovered in 1801, Ceres is the _____ dwarf planet to the Sun and is the only one located in the

_____ between the planets _____ and

_____. Ceres is the _____ of the Dwarf Planets,

and the only one without any moons. Ceres is named after the

Greek goddess of the Harvest, which is also where we get the

name cereal! Ceres has liquid water under its ice, which makes

it a candidate for life! Ceres takes _____ Earth Years to go

around the Sun, and _____ hours to rotate around.

Makemake: Makemake is the _____ furthest Dwarf

Planet from the Sun. Makemake is a beautiful shiny pink color,

believed to be frozen methane. Makemake has _____ moon,

named _____. Makemake takes _____ Earth Years to go

around the Sun, and _____ hours to rotate around.

Makemake is named after the Polynesian god of harvests.

Haumea: Haumea was discovered in 2004, and was

recognized as a Dwarf planet in 2008. Haumea has a

Weird _____. It is believed that _____.

It has by far the most rapid spin, taking only _____ hours to

complete a rotation. Haumea takes _____ Earth Years to go

around the Sun. Haumea has _____ moons. Names: ——————————

Pluto: Pluto was the first Kuiper Belt object discovered, Back in _____ it was originally thought to be the ninth planet. Pluto is named after _____. It is mostly made of ice and rock. It has _____ moons, although one of them, _____, is about half the size of pluto itself. One day on Pluto lasts _____ hours, while one year is _____ Earth Years.

Eris: Eris is the largest Dwarf Planet, and the reason why _____was made a Dwarf Planet. One day on Eris lasts _____ hours, while one year is _____ Earth Years. It is named after _____. Eris has _____ moon. It is named _____ after the goddess of lawlessness.

Comets

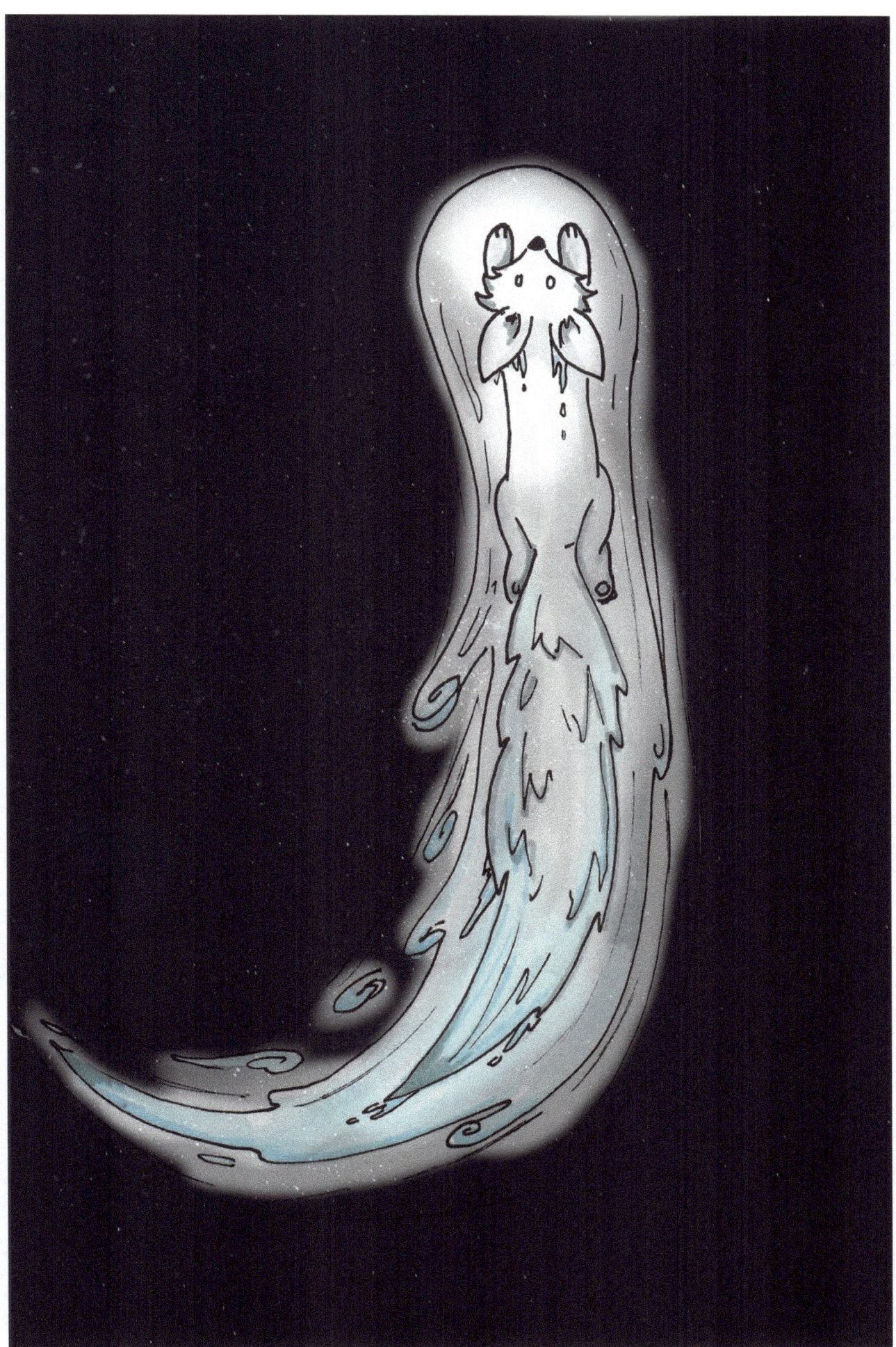

Meteor

Asteroid Belt

Kuiper Belt

Comets: comets are leftovers from the dawn of our solar system around 4.6 billion years ago, and consist mostly of ice coated with dark organic material. They have been referred to as "dirty snowballs." Each comet has a tiny frozen part, called a nucleus, often no larger than a few kilometers across. The nucleus contains icy chunks, frozen gases with bits of embedded dust. A comet warms up as it nears the Sun and develops an atmosphere, or coma. The Sun's heat causes the comet's ices to change to gases so the coma gets larger. The coma may extend hundreds of thousands of kilometers. The pressure of sunlight and high-speed solar particles (solar wind) can blow the coma dust and gas away from the Sun, sometimes forming a long, bright tail. Comets actually have two tails—a dust tail and an ion (gas) tail.

Most comets travel a safe distance from the Sun—comet Halley comes no closer than 89 million kilometers (55 million miles). However, some comets, called sungrazers, crash straight into the Sun or get so close that they break up and evaporate.

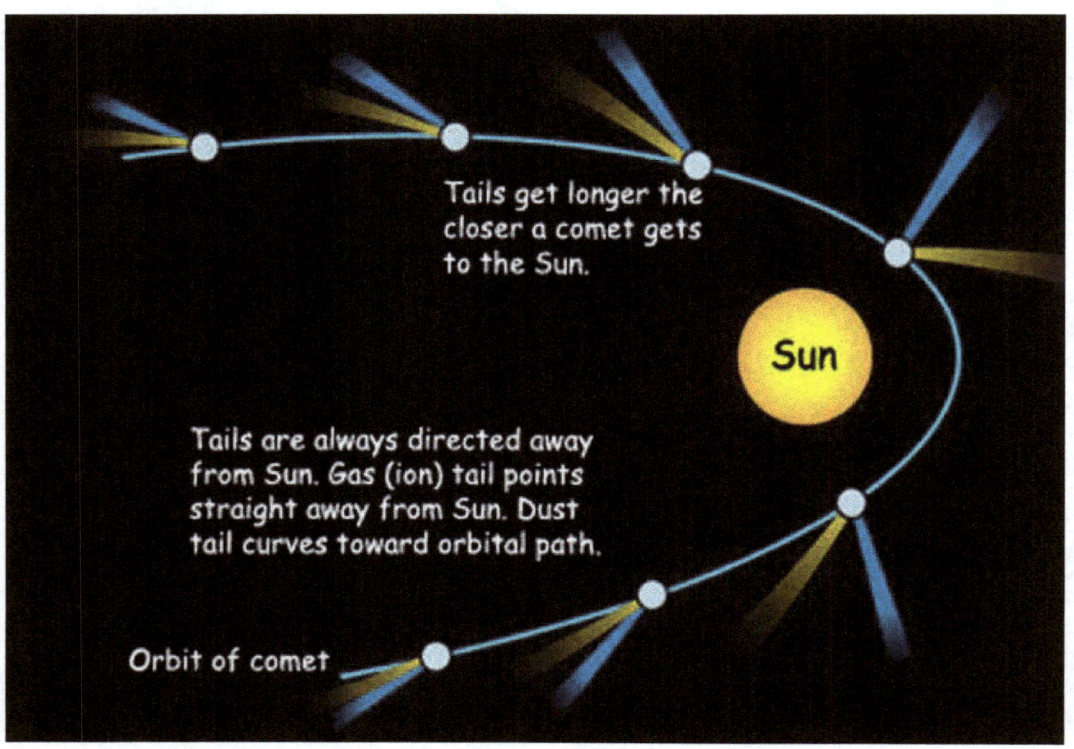

Tails get longer the closer a comet gets to the Sun.

Sun

Tails are always directed away from Sun. Gas (ion) tail points straight away from Sun. Dust tail curves toward orbital path.

Orbit of comet

What's that flash of light streaking across the sky? We call the objects that creates this brilliant effect by different names, depending on where it is.

Meteoroids are what we call "space rocks" that range in size from dust grains to small asteroids. This term only applies when they're in space.

Most are pieces of other, larger bodies that have been broken or blasted off. Some come from comets, others from asteroids, and some even come from the Moon and other planets. Some meteoroids are rocky, while others are metallic, or combinations of rock and metal.

When meteoroids enter Earth's atmosphere, or that of another planet, like Mars, at high speed and burn up, they're called **meteors**. This is also when we refer to them as shooting stars." Sometimes meteors can even appear brighter than Venus -- that's when we call them "fireballs." Scientists estimate that about 48.5 tons (44,000 kilograms) of meteoritic material falls on Earth each day.

When a meteoroid survives its trip through the atmosphere and hits the ground, it's called a **meteorite**.

Several meteors per hour can usually be seen on any given night. When there are lots more meteors, you're watching a **meteor shower**. Some meteor showers occur annually or at regular intervals as the Earth passes through the trail of dusty debris left by a comet and, in a few cases, asteroids).

Corvus, Bootes, Lupus, Centaurus

How to Draw Corvus

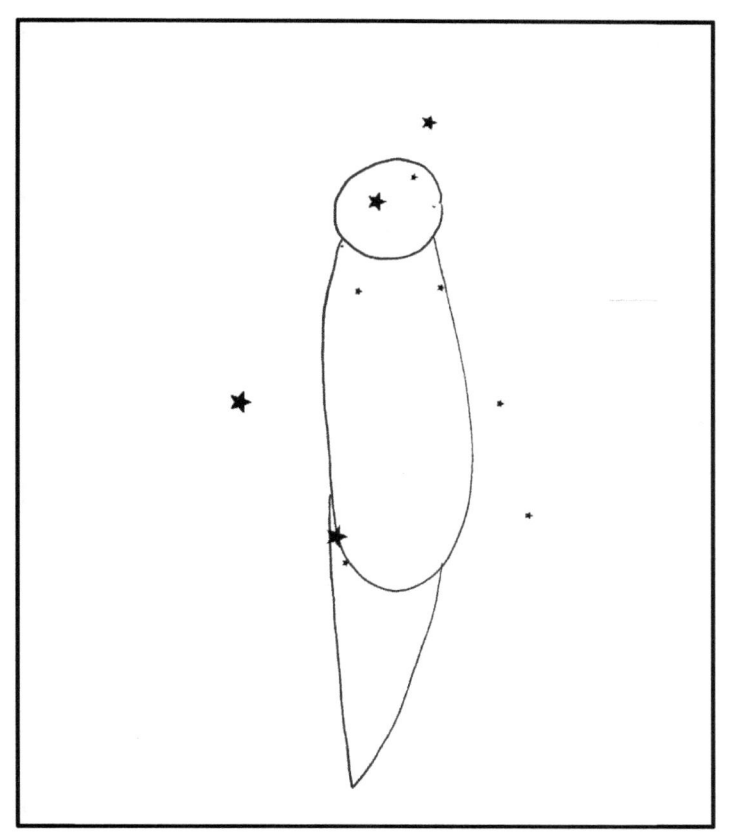
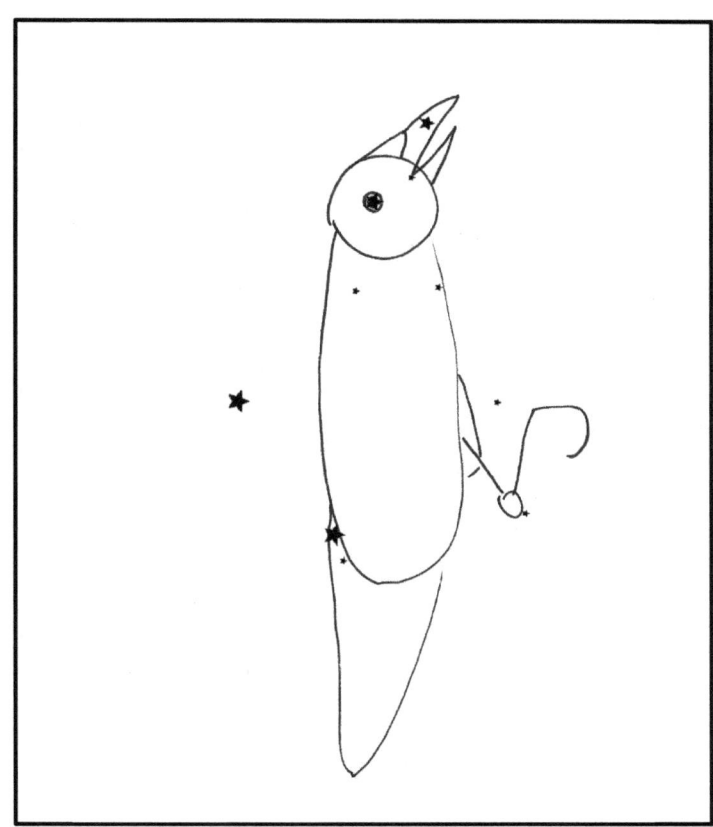

How to Draw Bootes

How to Draw Centaurus and Lupus

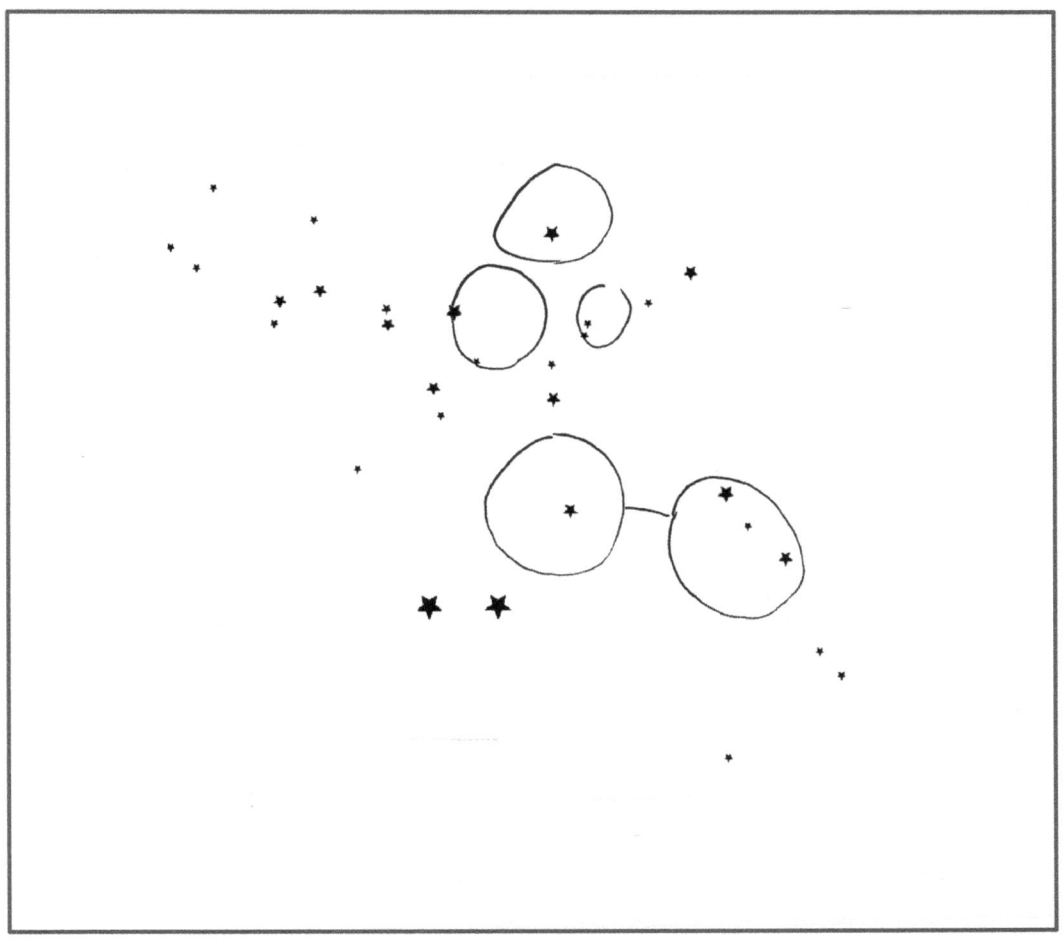

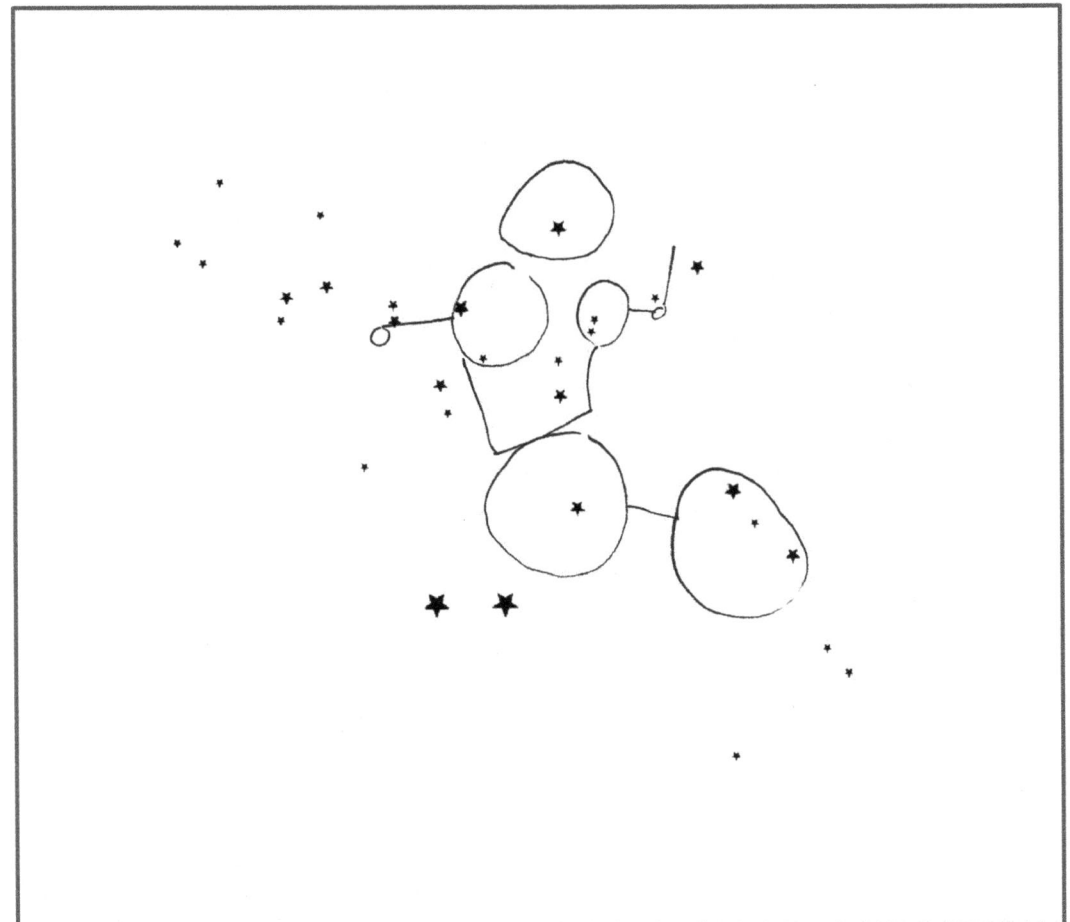

How to Draw Centaurus and Lupus

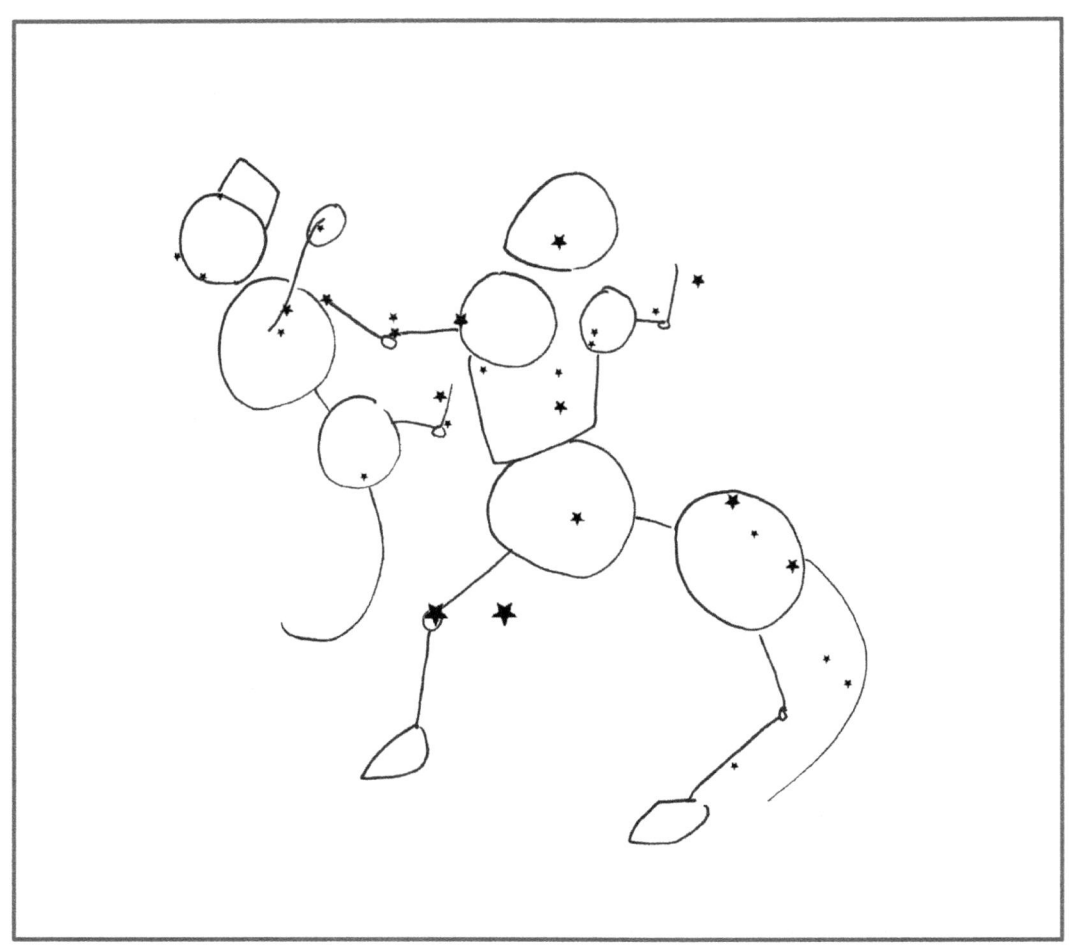

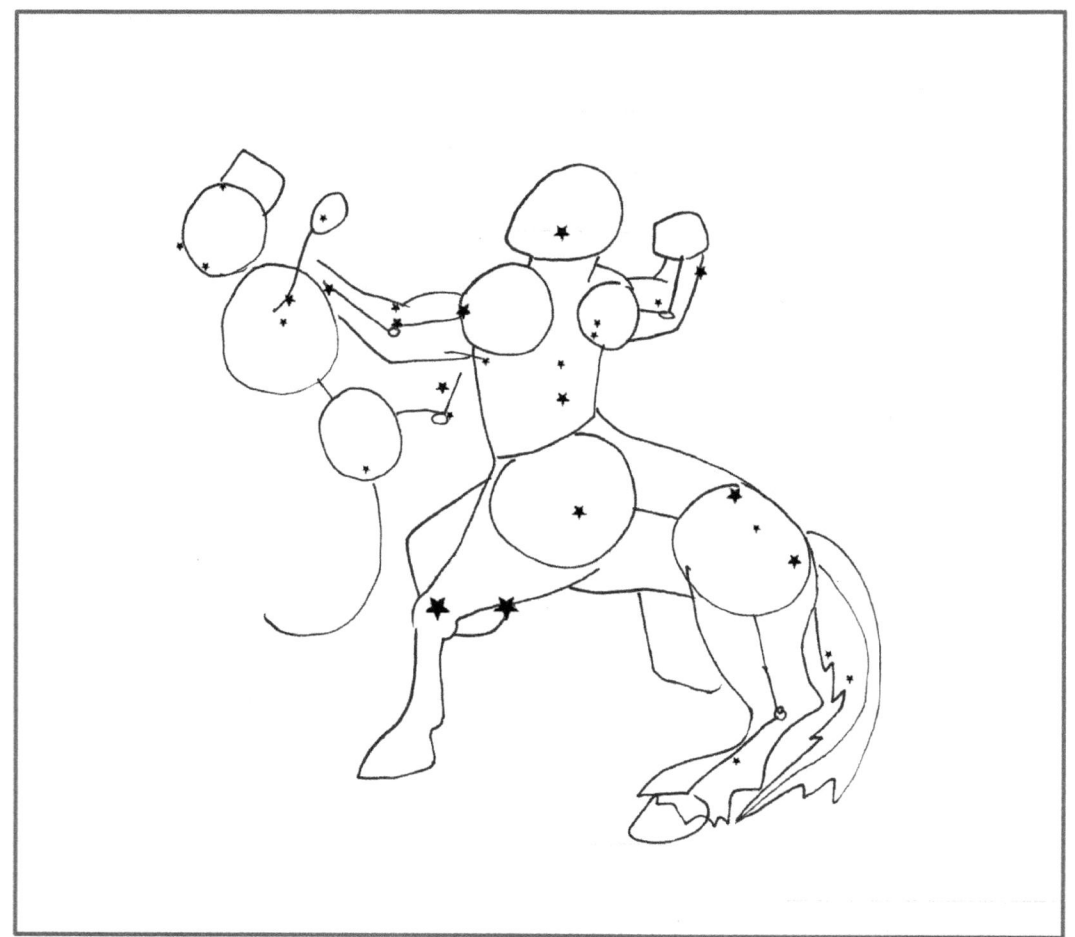

How to Draw Centaurus and Lupus

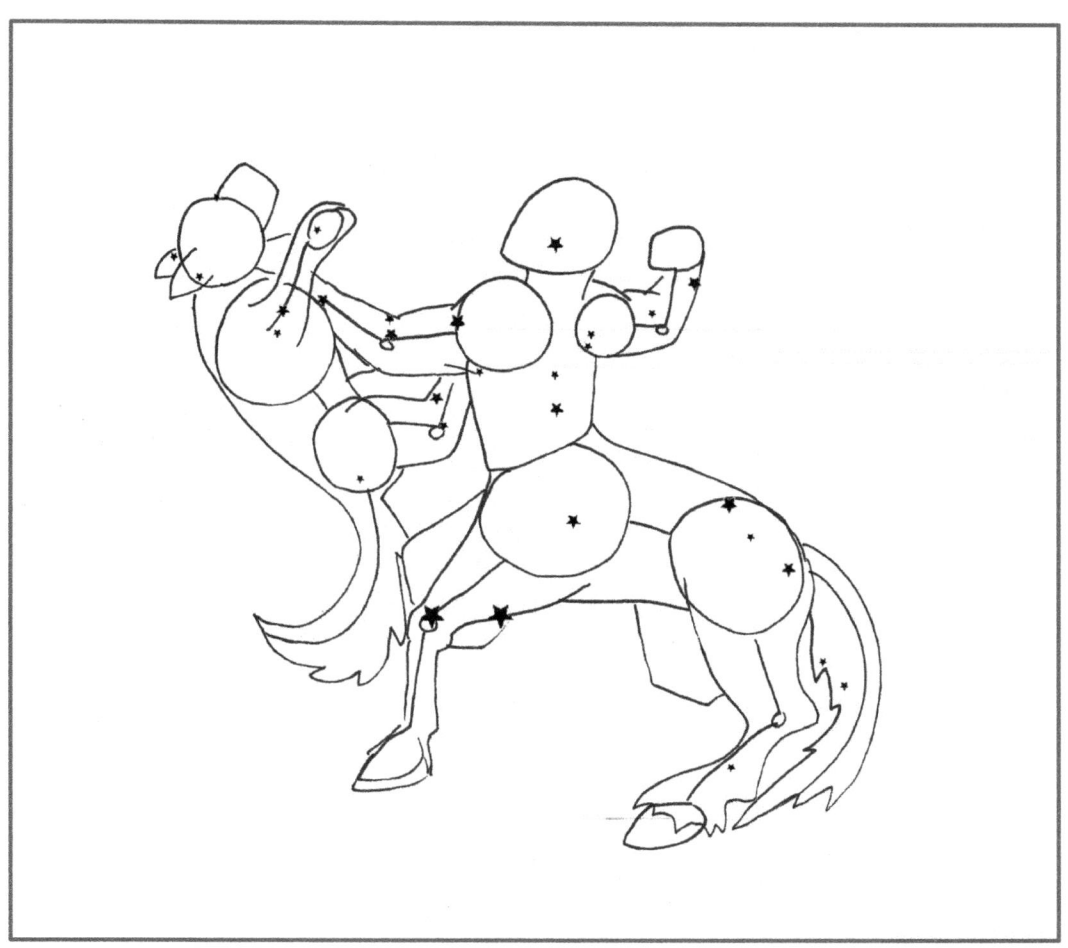

Practice Drawing

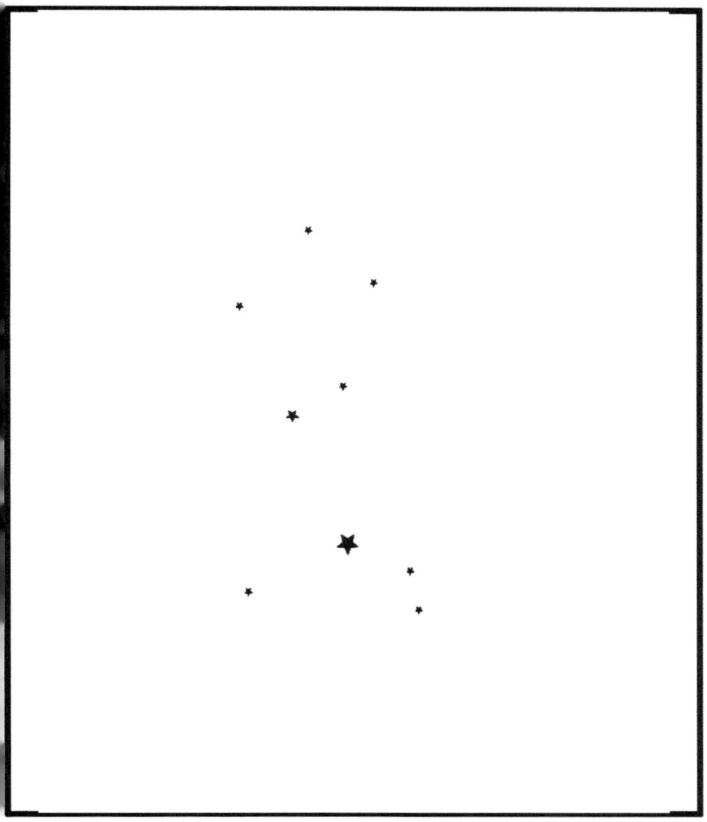

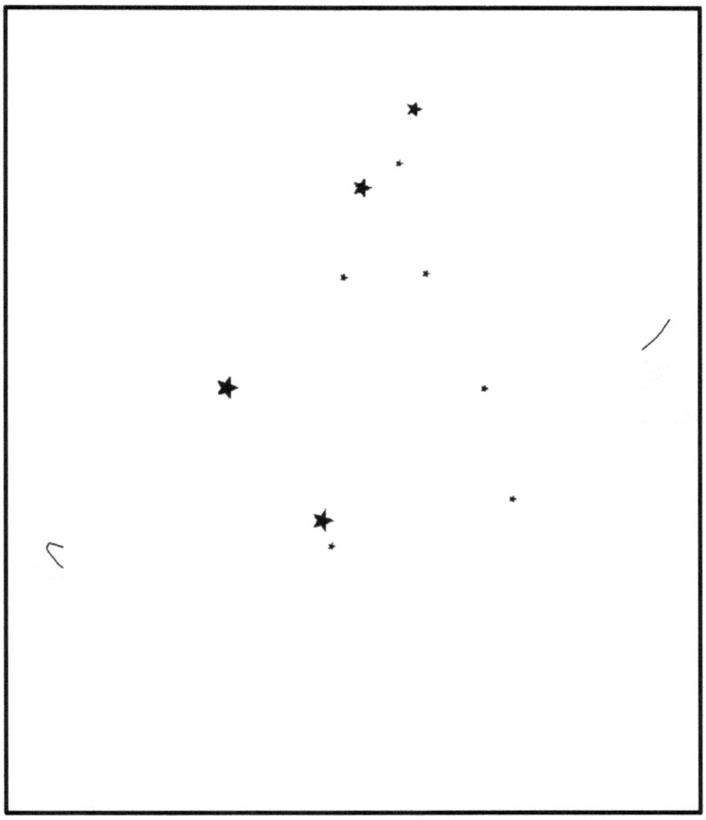

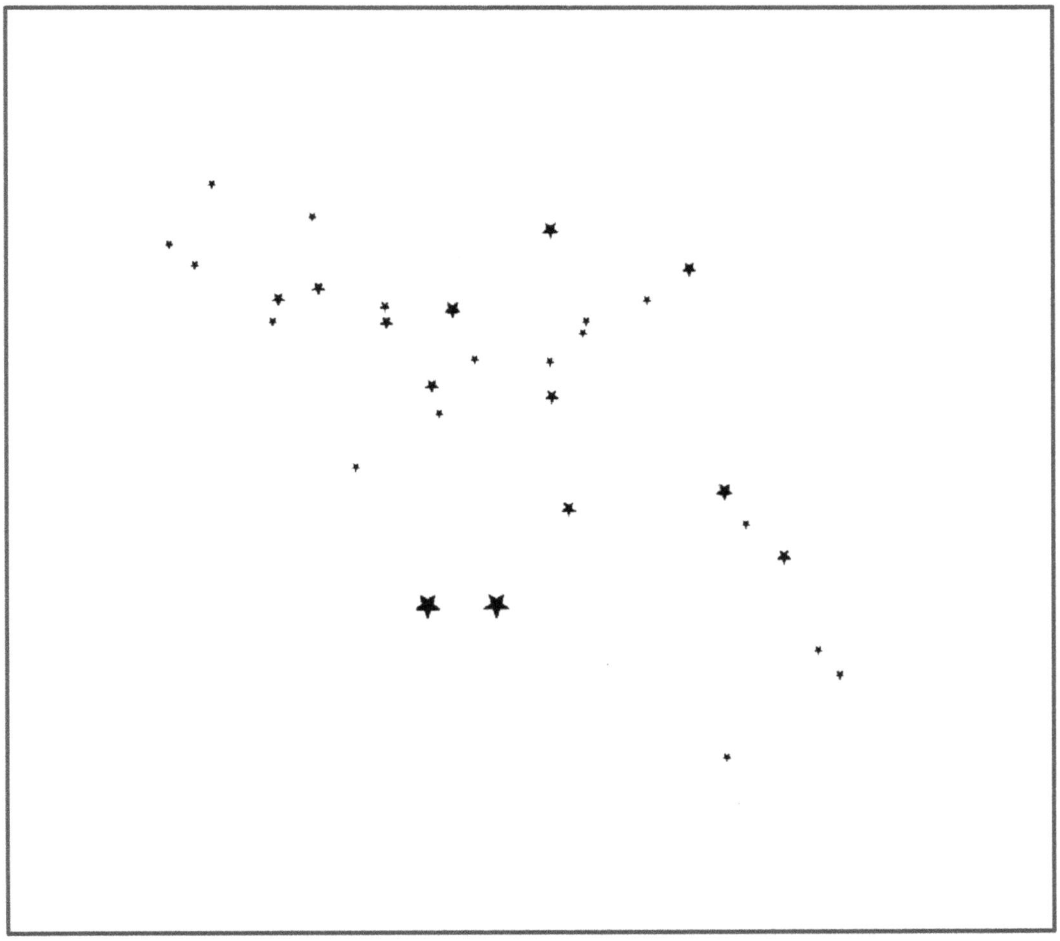

Homework Drawing

I was able to see: ☐ Bootes ☐ Corvus ☐ Lupus ☐ Centaurus

Zodiac pt.4

Zodiac pt.4

How to Draw Libra

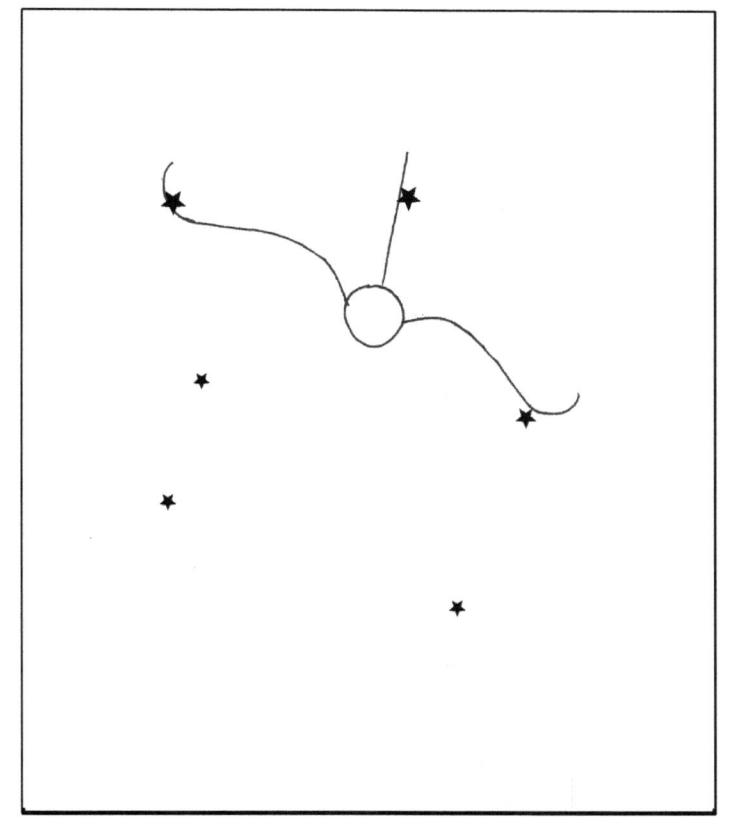

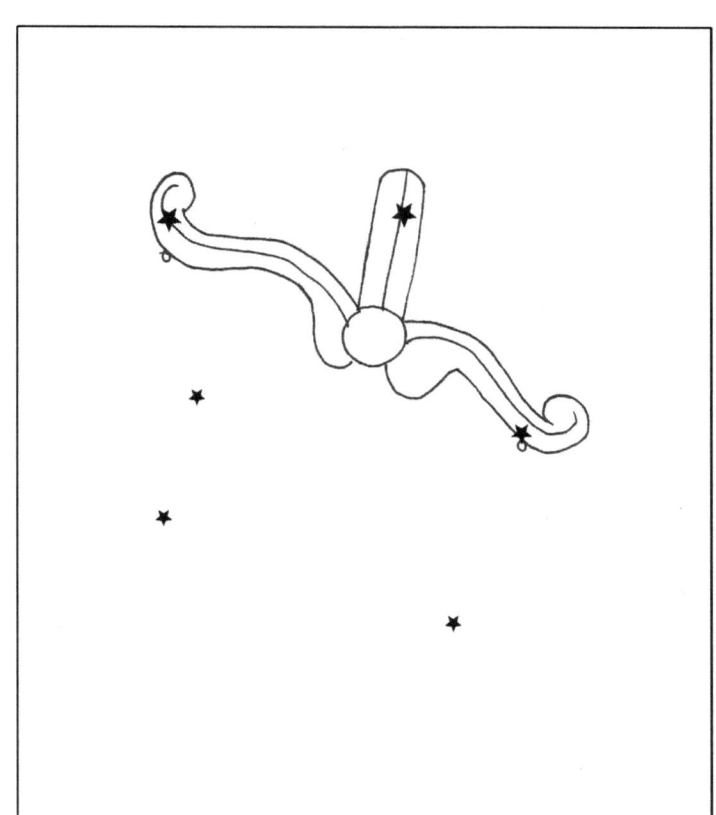

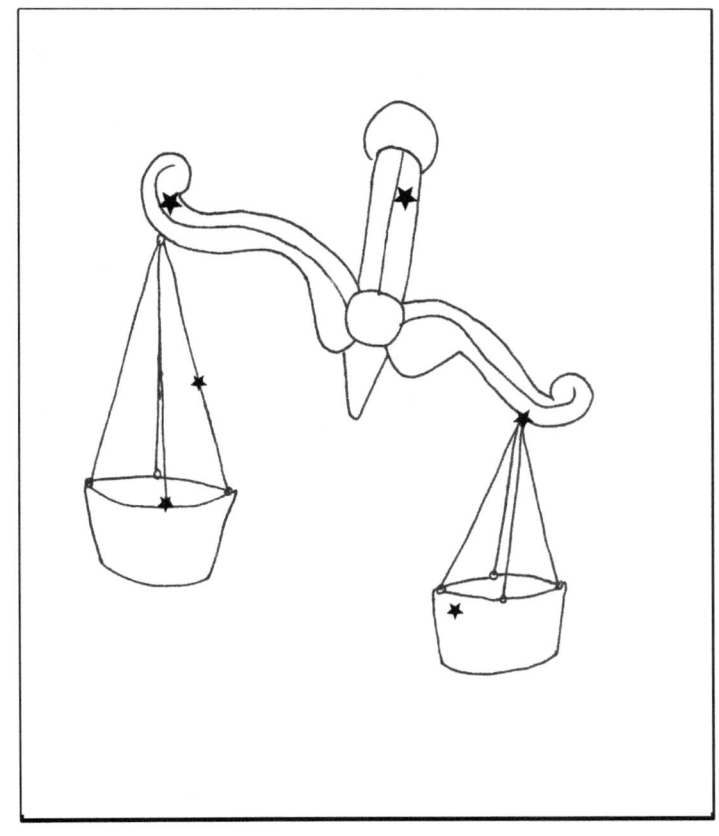

How to Draw Leo

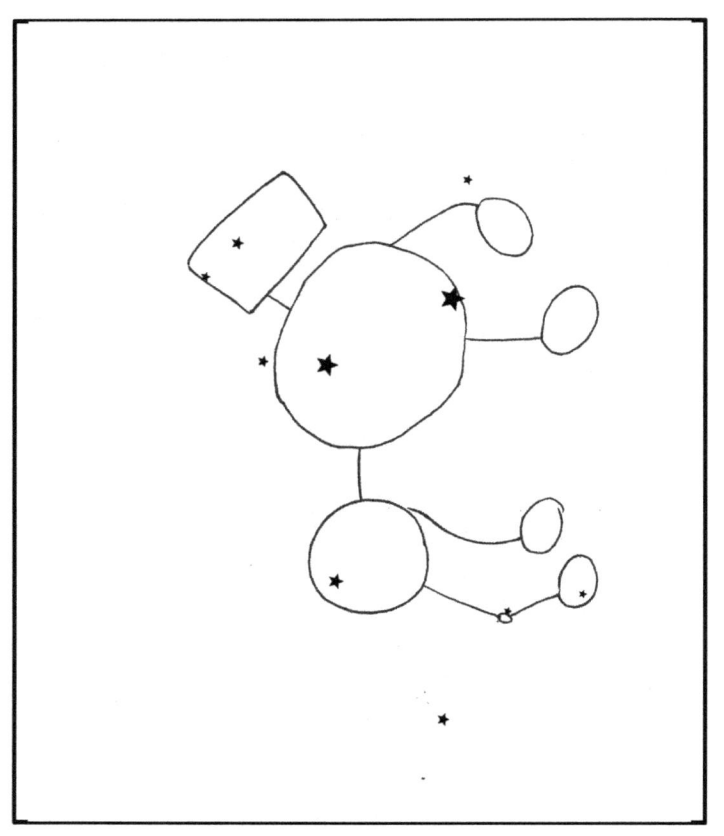

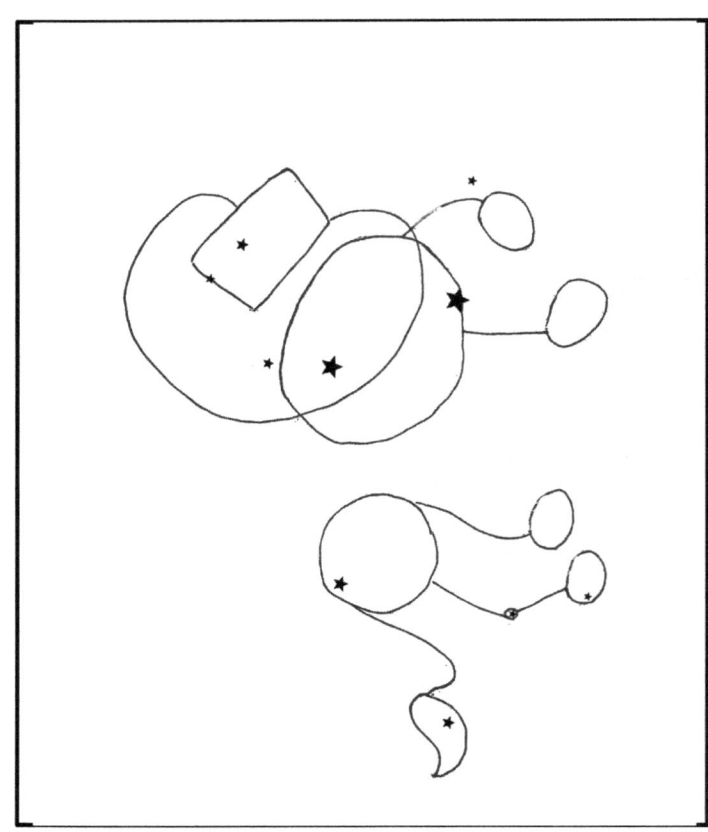

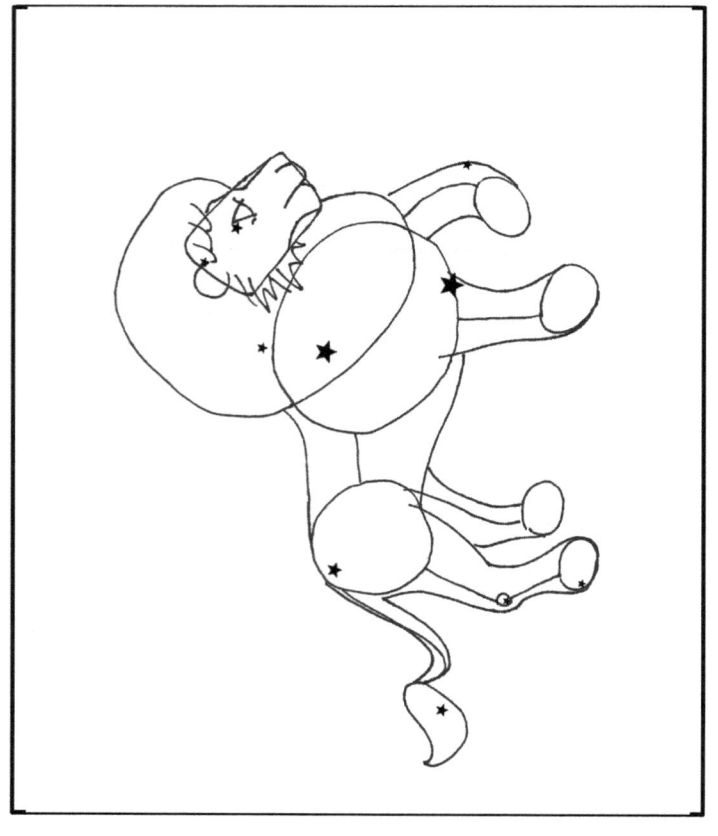

How to Draw Virgo

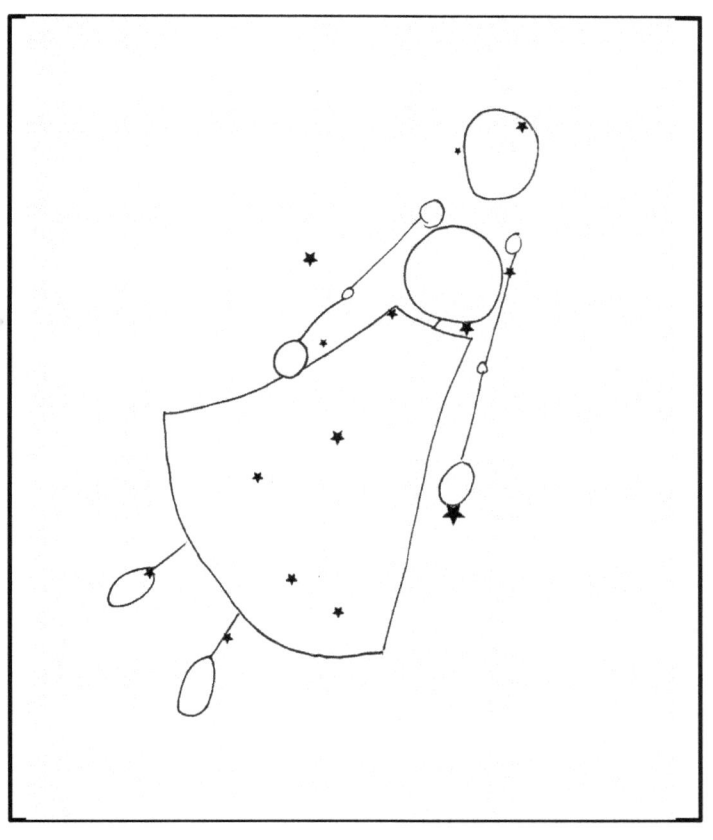

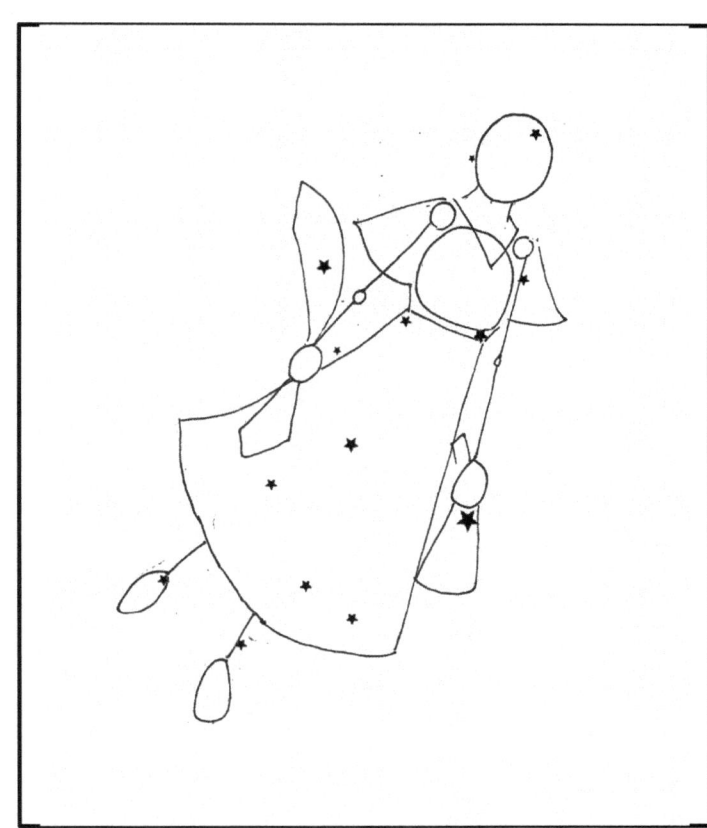

Practice Drawing

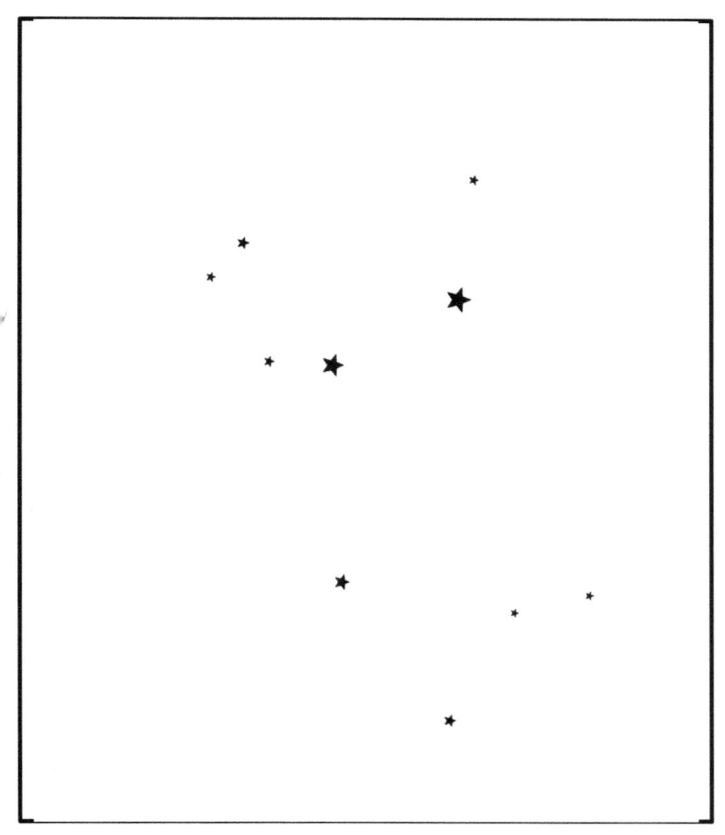

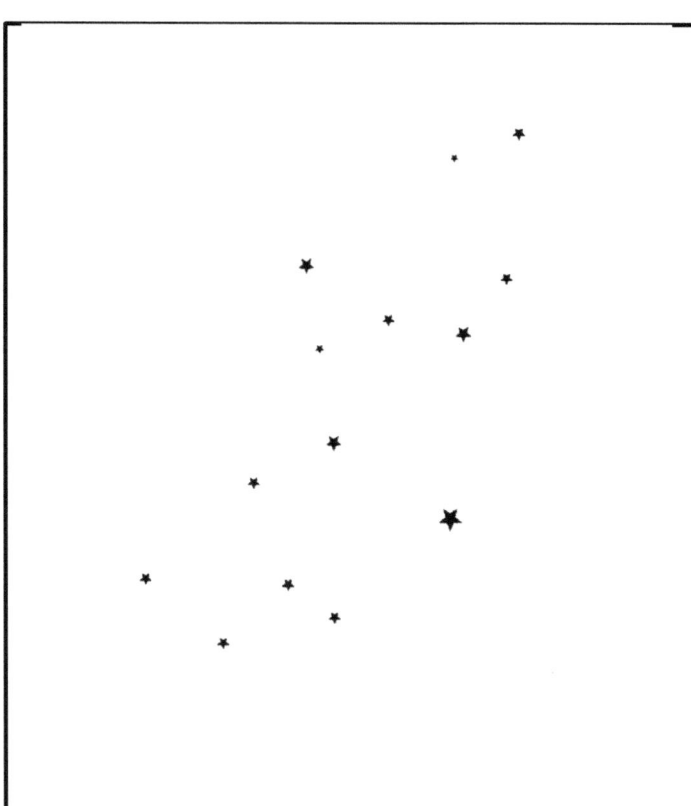

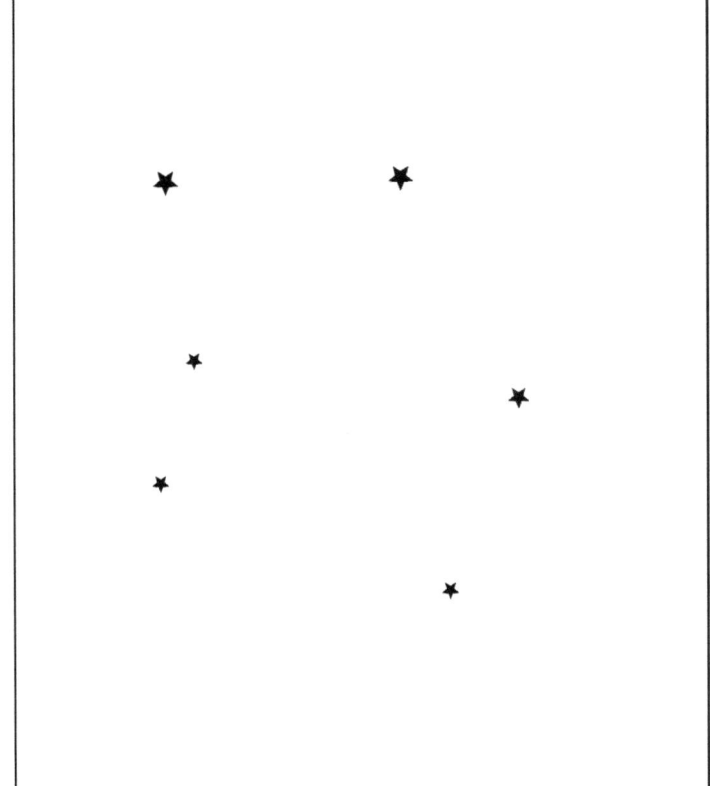

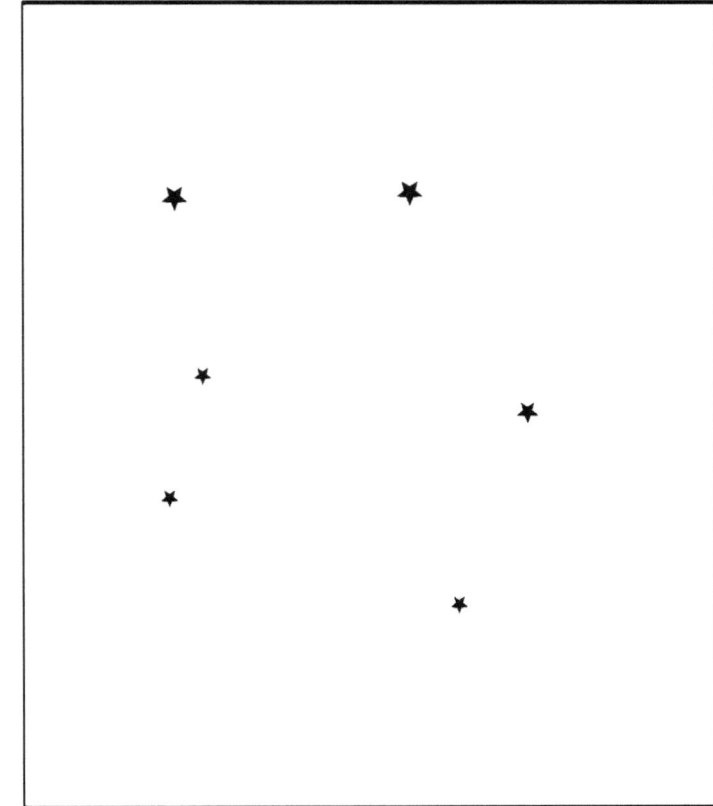

Homework Drawing

I was able to see: ☐ Libra ☐ Leo ☐ Virgo

Make sure to identify the constellations!

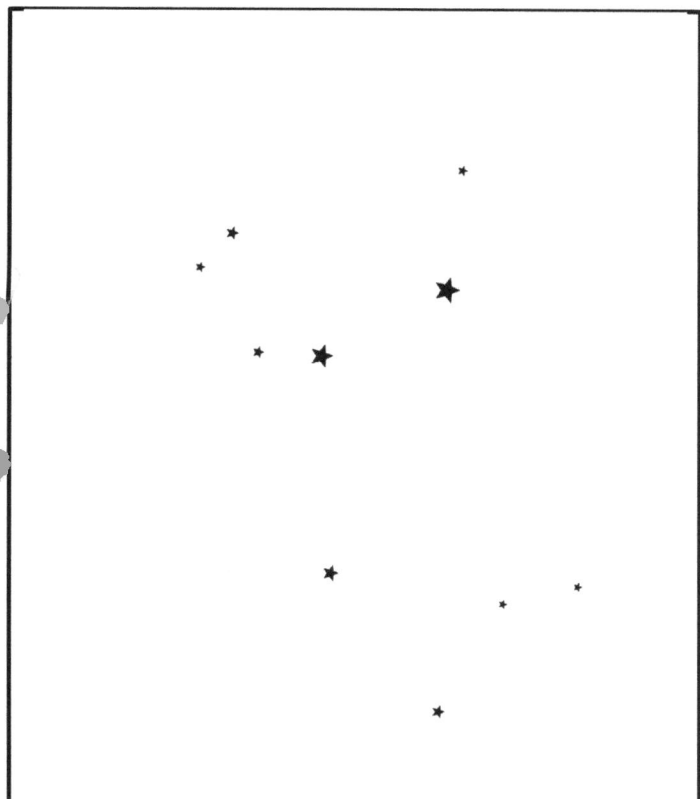

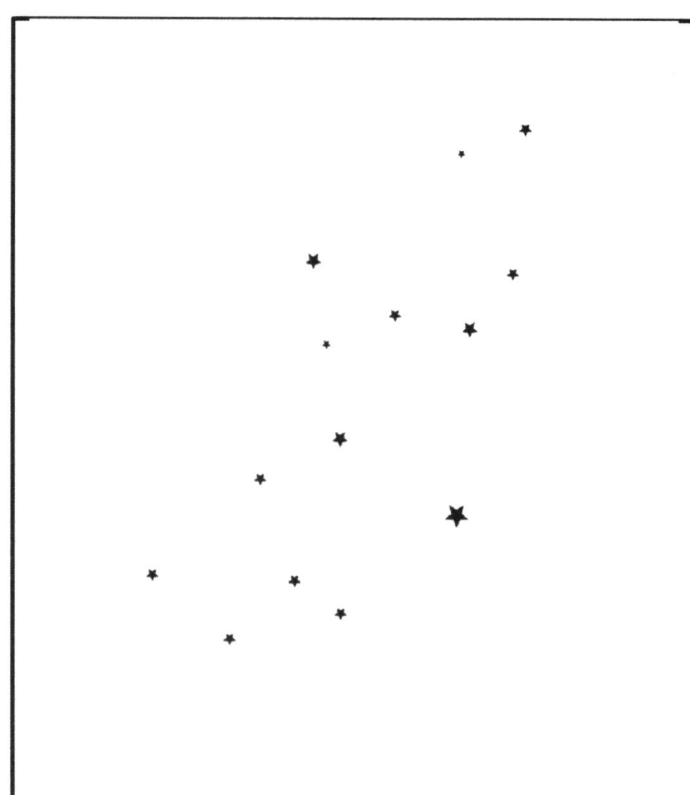

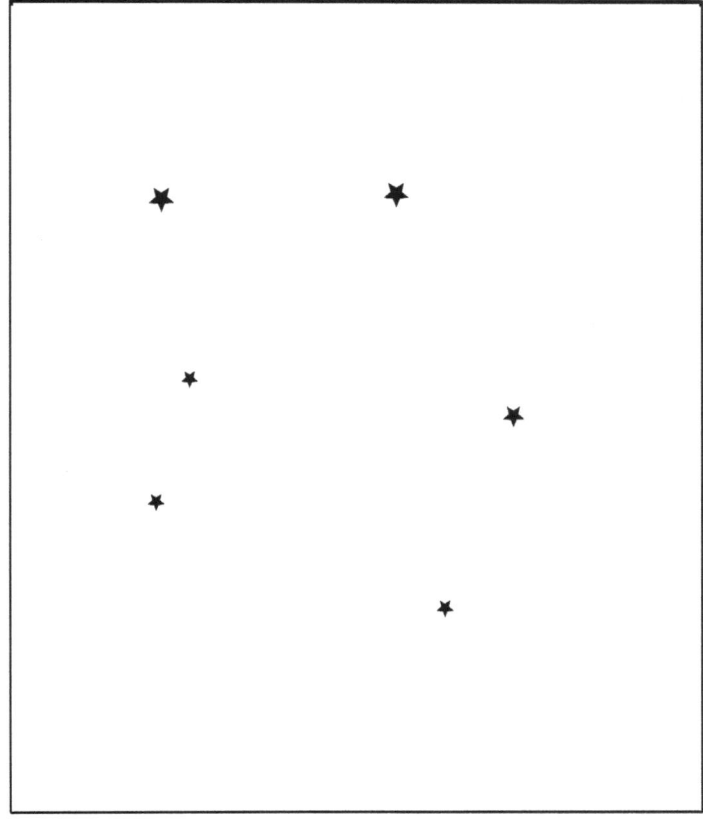

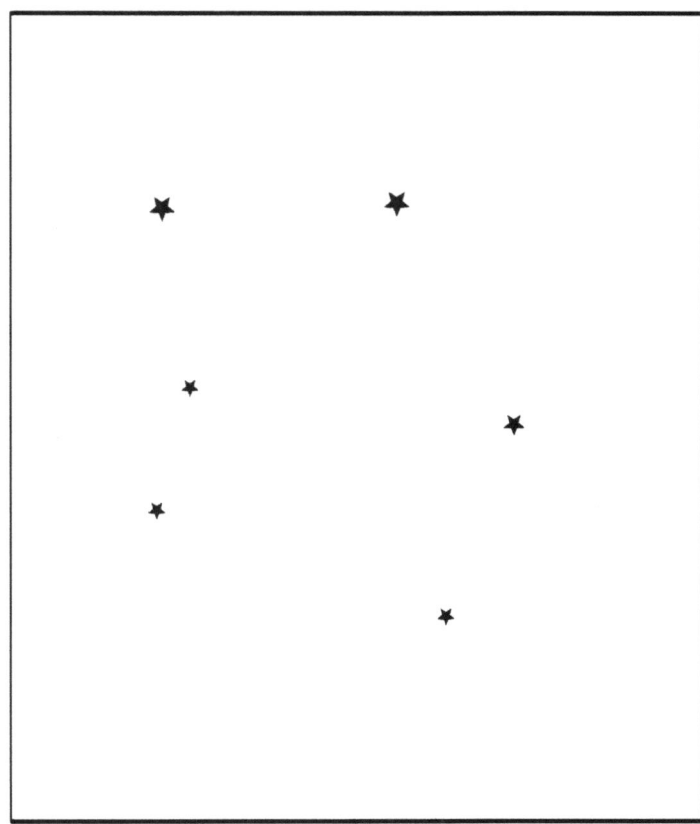

9 781088 048597